"Mark Boyer offers some very useful stats about the biblical text used in the Roman Catholic Lectionary. Additionally, he suggests possible alternative readings for inclusion in this Lectionary."

—**Pauline Nugent**, professor emerita of classics,
Missouri State University

"Mark Boyer has produced a welcome analysis of the Roman Catholic Lectionary that both critiques and supplements that tool for those who wish to amplify their sermons, provide wider context to Bible study, or simply need a further aid in working through the biblical text throughout the year. Taken together, the Lectionary and Boyer's volume provide more complete coverage and an opportunity to expand personal and group study."

—**Victor H. Matthews**, professor emeritus of religious studies,
Missouri State University

"Nearly sixty-one years after the liturgical renewal began, we now have a book that is honest about the Bible and how it is used in liturgy. As a preacher and teacher, I have struggled to connect biblical texts to their liturgical use, and so this book makes a significant contribution to making full use of the Bible in the church, both in liturgy and continuing Bible studies in parishes."

—**Vernon Meyer**, adjunct professor of theology,
Grand Canyon University

"Noting the Lectionary's omission of large portions of the Bible, Mark Boyer proposes an alternative series of passages. Individuals wishing to read all the books of the Bible during designated seasons over a course of several years will find his work useful."

—**Paul Turner**, pastor, Cathedral of the Immaculate Conception

"Once again, Mark Boyer has turned his attention to a book that I deal with every day as a priest, but have never given much thought to taking apart and examining its construction—the Roman Catholic Lectionary! It is interesting to have at my fingertips facts about what pieces of the Scriptures we read in our yearly cycles, and which books get left out! Even more intriguing is the question of, 'Why?' Agree with his theories or not, the author always makes me think, which is why I often pick up copies of his works."

—**John Friedel**, pastor and certified campus minster, Diocese of Springfield-Cape Girardeau

The Roman Catholic Lectionary and the Bible

The Roman Catholic Lectionary and the Bible

Analysis, Conclusions, Suggested Alternatives

The *Lectionary* and the *Bible*

Mark G. Boyer

WIPF & STOCK · Eugene, Oregon

THE ROMAN CATHOLIC LECTIONARY AND THE BIBLE
Analysis, Conclusions, Suggested Alternatives

Wipf & Stock
An Imprint of Wipf and Stock Publishers
199 W. 8th Ave., Suite 3
Eugene, OR 97401

www.wipfandstock.com

PAPERBACK ISBN: 979-8-3852-1933-9
HARDCOVER ISBN: 979-8-3852-1934-6
EBOOK ISBN: 979-8-3852-1935-3

VERSION NUMBER 06/24/24

Dedicated to

Noah Joseph Casey

(1949–2015),

classmate, friend, monk,

spiritual guide, diocesan priest.

. . . [I]t is out of the word of God handed down in writing that even now "God speaks to his people" . . . .

—"Introduction," par 12

Proclamation is not . . . "about God" but reveals God.

—Meyer, "Preacher," 70

The *Lectionary* and the *Bible*

Contents

The *Lectionary* and the *Bible*

Abbreviations

BCE = Before the Common Era (same as BC = Before Christ)

CB (NT) = Christian Bible (New Testament)

Acts = Acts of the Apostles

Col = Letter to the Colossians

1 Cor = First Letter of Paul to the Corinthians

2 Cor = Second Letter of Paul to the Corinthians

Eph = Letter to the Ephesians

Gal = Letter of Paul to the Galatians

Heb = Letter to the Hebrews

Jas = Letter of James

John = John's Gospel

1 John = First Letter of John

2 John = Second Letter of John

3 John = Third Letter of John

Jude = Letter of Jude

Luke = Luke's Gospel

Mark = Mark's Gospel

Matt = Matthew's Gospel

1 Pet = First Letter of Peter

2 Pet = Second Letter of Peter

Phil = Letter of Paul to the Philippians

Phlm = Letter of Paul to Philemon

Rev = Revelation

Rom = Letter of Paul to the Romans

1 Thess = First Letter of Paul to the Thessalonians

2 Thess = Second Letter to the Thessalonians

1 Tim = First Letter to Timothy

2 Tim = Second Letter to Timothy

Titus = Letter to Titus

CE = Common Era (same as AD = *Anno Domini*, in the year of the Lord)

HB (OT) = Hebrew Bible (Old Testament)

Amos = Amos

1 Chr = First Book of Chronicles

2 Chr = Second Book of Chronicles

Dan = Daniel

Deut = Deuteronomy

Eccl – Ecclesiastes

Esth = Esther

Exod = Exodus

Ezek = Ezekiel

Ezra = Ezra

Gen = Genesis

Hab = Habakkuk

Hag = Haggai

Hos = Hosea

Isa = Isaiah

Jer = Jeremiah

Job = Job

Joel = Joel

Jonah = Jonah

Josh = Joshua

Judg = Judges

1 Kgs = First Book of Kings

2 Kgs = Second Book of Kings

Lam = Lamentations

Lev = Leviticus

Mal = Malachi

Mic = Micah

Nah = Nahum

Neh = Nehemiah

Num = Numbers

Obad = Obadiah

Prov = Proverbs

Ps(s) = Psalm(s)

Ruth = Ruth

1 Sam = First Book of Samuel

2 Sam = Second Book of Samuel

Song = Song of (Solomon) Songs

Zech = Zechariah

Zeph = Zephaniah

OT (A) = Old Testament (Apocrypha)

Bar = Baruch

Bel = Bell and the Dragon

Ep Jer = Epistle (Letter) of Jeremiah

Jdt = Judith

1 Macc = Frist Book of Maccabees

2 Macc = Second Book of Maccabees

Sir = Sirach (Ecclesiasticus)

Tob = Tobit

Wis = Wisdom (of Solomon)

par(s) = paragraph(s)

Punctuation Usage for Biblical Notations

: = chapter (left of :), verses (right of :) (5:1–5)

– = range of verses within a chapter of a biblical book (5:1–5)

— = range of verses within chapters of a biblical book (5:1—7:3)

, = separates ranges of verses within a chapter of a biblical book (5:13, 6–8, 11–13)

; = separates ranges of verses within a biblical book (5:1–5; 7:1–3; 8:12–13)

a, b, c = designates first (a), second (b), third (c), etc. sentence in a verse of Scripture or lines of poetic text (5:1b–5; 7:1–3b)

Introduction

Vatican Council II and the Lectionary

In "The Constitution on the Sacred Liturgy," issued December 4, 1963, the bishops attending the Second Vatican Council (1962–65) decreed: "The treasures of the Bible are to be opened up more lavishly so that a richer fare may be provided for the faithful at the table of God's word."[1] The goal was to present "a more representative part of the sacred scripture . . . to the people in the course of a prescribed number of years."[2] After a committee was appointed to provide directions for a series of readings in 1969,[3] the first volume—of what ultimately became four volumes plus a supplement in English—was published in Latin on September 30, 1970, with the other volumes following in subsequent years. The "Dogmatic Constitution on Divine Revelation," issued November 18, 1965, spurred the study of Scripture with its endorsement of the form-critical method.[4]

---

1. "Constitution," par 51.
2. "Constitution," par 51.
3. Turner, *Words*, 1–42.
4. "Dogmatic Constitution," pars 11–20.

A lectionary is a book that contains a collection of biblical texts appointed for worship on given days; the word *lectionary* comes from the word *lection*, meaning *a biblical passage assigned to be read (heard) on a particular day*. The Christian lectionary developed from the Jewish lectionary, the practice of reading a prescribed text on the Sabbaths during a year. Before Vatican II (1962–65), the Roman Catholic Lectionary consisted of a one-year set of biblical texts assigned to every day of the year.

After the close of Vatican II, the decision was made—in light of the "Constitution on the Sacred Liturgy's" decree that a richer fare from the Bible be provided to people—to create a Lectionary for Sundays that recurred on a three-year cycle and a Lectionary for Weekdays that recurred on a two-year cycle. Each Sunday cycle consists of four biblical texts: (1) a HB (OT) passage—called the First Reading—chosen to echo something in the gospel passage, (2) a Responsorial Psalm, a few verses from a biblical Psalm with a refrain echoing the First Reading, (3) a biblical passage from a CB (NT) letter, read (heard) on a semi-continuous basis from one Sunday to the next, and (4) a passage from a Gospel preceded by a sung Alleluia and a verse that presents a theme from the Gospel about to be read (heard). Gospel passages are chosen according to a repeating three-year cycle: Year A (Matthew) 2023, 2026, etc.; Year B (Mark), 2024, 2027, etc.; and Year C (Luke), 2025, 2028, etc.

The Weekday Lectionary is divided into Year I (odd numbered years) and Year II (even numbered years). The gospel passages are the same for both Year I and Year II. The First Reading consists of continuous or (most often) semi-continuous pericopes from both HB (OT) and CB (NT) books which differ. Thus, while the gospel pericopes are the same for Year I and Year II, the First Readings are not the same, but they repeat every other year.

For a history of the Lectionary's coming into existence and its development, Paul Turner provides the story in *Words without Alloy: A Biography of the Lectionary for Mass*.[5] These 286-pages present the background concerning the idea of the current Roman Catholic Lectionary, then individual sections on the Sundays

---

5. Collegeville, MN: Liturgical Press Academic, 2022.

and Solemnities in the Sunday Cycles and the sections on the two Weekday Years. In the last section, titled "Concluding Observations," Turner offers reflections on both the positive consequences of the Lectionary—such as its impact on liturgical, catechetical, and pastoral life—and concerns—such as its minimal biblical accounts featuring women and harmonization of HB (OT) pericopes with CB (NT) gospel passages.

Once the Roman Catholic Lectionary was issued, it inspired the publication of a lectionary by the Consultation on Church Union in 1974, the Common Lectionary of 1983, and the Revised Common Lectionary in 1994. After the first edition of the Roman Catholic Lectionary was completed, issued, and prepared in English in a single volume in 1970, the second edition began to appear in 1998 with Volume I for *Sundays, Solemnities, Feasts of the Lord and Saints*; Volume II, *Proper of Seasons for Weekdays, Year I, Proper of Saints, Common of Saints* in 2002; Volume III, *Proper of Seasons for Weekdays, Year II, Proper of Saints, Common of Saints* in 2002; Volume IV, *Common of Saints, Ritual Masses for Various Needs and Occasions, Votive Masses, and Masses for the Dead* in 2002; *Book of the Gospels* in 2001, and *Supplement* in 2017. The latter volume represents updates from 1998 and 2002 to 2017. The result of people seeing these volumes consisting of more pages than most Bibles was the Roman Catholic's erroneous thinking that he or she heard (read) the whole Bible every three years! Nothing could be further from the truth as is pointed out below in this book.

This Author's Concerns: This Book

It is important to note that those who made decisions about what biblical material to include in the Lectionary also made decisions about what biblical material to exclude. In other words, the Lectionary edits the Bible. People who study the Lectionary pericopes often call their activity Bible Study; the fact that it is Lectionary Study eludes them.

The Bible has been used in the Lectionary to support the biases of the editors. This is true in particular of the HB (OT) used in Sunday Cycle A, B, and C; the passages chosen are meant to echo something in the gospel pericope. It is also pronounced during Weekdays Year I and II, when analyzing what has been omitted when semi-continuous passages are presented. Oftentimes, the valuable introductory material to both the HB (OT) and the CB (NT) books—usually found in chapter 1 of the book—has been omitted.

While the Sunday Cycle A, B, and C boasts that the Second Reading is semi-continuous from one Sunday to the next, an analysis shows that much has been omitted between the semi-continuous passages! Likewise, the gospels are presented as semi-continuous, but important material—often unique—has been omitted.

Weekdays I and II present semi-continuous passages from both a biblical book other than a gospel and from a gospel. In many cases, only a selection has been made. In some instances, as will be seen in the following chapters, only one or two passages from a given biblical book can be found in the Lectionary.

Thus, what is read (heard) on Sundays consists of a very small selection of biblical material. Add to that what is read (heard) on Weekdays, and there is still very little of the Bible presented over two or three years. Indeed, if a Bible were printed from Lectionary texts, it would be about one-third or less of the size of a printed English Bible today.

Furthermore, the Lectionary represents the editing of biblical books, no matter if it be history, wisdom, or prophet. When parts of a biblical book are left out of the Lectionary, those that are included form a new biblical book that does not exist! Similarly, put all edited biblical books together and there is a Bible within a Bible that does not exist!

Especially on Sundays, the HB (OT) pericope is always out of context. Just like one would not take a novel, open it to page 132, read the first paragraph, and proceed to explain what the paragraph meant, one should not take a passage from the prophet

Isaiah, chapter 53, read it, and explain what it means without understanding its context in Isaiah 53, along with what precedes
it and what follows it. The meaning of a biblical passage—or a
paragraph from any book—is dependent upon its context in the
book in which it appears.

The Lectionary maintains translation biases. For example, CB
(NT) often presents Jesus Christ or Christ Jesus. Christ is a Greek
word that has not been translated. In Greek, *christ* means *anointed*.
Thus, translations of Jesus Christ should be Jesus Anointed, and
translations of Christ Jesus should be Anointed Jesus. Kings of
Judah and Israel were anointed with oil. The prophet Isaiah calls
the Persian King Cyrus an anointed! The connotation is that the
anointed one has responded to a call from God.

Biblical topics that may offend modern readers are omitted.
God's anger and wrath are seldom presented, nor is slavery and
other such topics that modern people don't like reading (hearing).
Powerful biblical women are ignored.

Biblical prophetic books are chopped by piecing together
verses, which not only create a pericope that does not exist in the
prophetic book in the Bible, but creates a new prophetic book.
Also, there is a heavy emphasis on messianic texts in prophetic
literature.

While there are multiple pericopes about the exile of the
Jews from Israel to Assyria and the exile of the Jews from Judah
to Babylon, there are few passages narrating the return of the Jews
from Babylonian exile.

There does not seem to be an application of modern biblical analysis—called the historical-critical method—as presented
in the "Dogmatic Constitution on Divine Revelation," especially
paragraphs 11 through 26. Indeed, the Lectionary seems to ig-
nore modern biblical scholarship. For example, biblical scholars
no longer equate the beloved disciple in John's Gospel with the
name of the author: John. The beloved disciple is never named.
Instead of a single author named John the Apostle, most biblical scholars think that John's Gospel was created by a group of
writers, usually referred to as a school. Also, modern scholarship

divides the Pauline collections of letters between those thought to be authentic Paul and those thought to be second-generation Paul. In other words, while it looks like Paul wrote Romans, 1 Corinthians, 2 Corinthians, Galatians, and others, biblical scholars think that someone else wrote Ephesians, Colossians, and 2 Thessalonians, and put Paul's name on them. Thus, when the Lectionary states: "A reading from the letter of St. Paul to the Ephesians," it is claiming what is not true.

Often, Lectionary pericopes will begin with a pronoun—he, she, it, they—without supplying the noun—David, Ruth, water, Israelites—to which the pronoun refers. It is the responsibility of the reader (hearer) to attempt to figure out the antecedent of the pronoun.

Furthermore, there is no liturgical season when all the biblical passages presented in the Lectionary are read, because feasts and solemnities—which frequently interrupt liturgical seasons—have their own set of biblical passages to be proclaimed from the Lectionary. For example, during the Season of Lent, the solemnities of the Annunciation and St. Joseph interrupt the daily readings of Lent. Likewise, the Season of Advent is interrupted by feasts and solemnities and memorials—all of which have their own Lectionary-assigned passages—that supersede the daily passages found in the Lectionary for Advent. Thus, even though a biblical passage may be assigned to a given day that does not mean that it is heard (read) that day; in the Lectionary, the Solemnity of the Immaculate Conception of the Blessed Virgin Mary replaces the assigned texts no matter what day (except Sunday) and in what week of Advent it falls. There are other such kinds of interruptions; let it be stated that the table of Scriptures assigned by the Lectionary to every day of the year does not mean that a feast's, solemnity's, memorial's, or optional memorial's assigned biblical texts do not replace the daily assigned Scriptures.

The biblical passages presented in the Lectionary have been chosen to fit the liturgical year, even though the liturgical year did not exist when the Bible was written. Even though Eileen Schuller is correct when she writes that one result of Vatican Council II was "[a] renewed emphasis on the place of the Bible within Catholic life,"[6] she is incorrect when she writes that the Lectionary "provides the faithful with a knowledge of the whole of God's Word."[7] In her over-positive article about the Lectionary, she fails to note how much of the Bible is not in the Lectionary.

Other critiques of the Lectionary can be found in the chapters that follow.

This Book's Purpose

The purpose of this book is to present some sobering statistics about the biblical texts found in the Roman Catholic Lectionary along with a list of biblical texts not found in the Lectionary. It is also the goal of this book to propose Bible study of the biblical texts not found in the Lectionary by presenting them in cycles that imitate cycles found in the Lectionary. Thus, there are four alternative sets of First Readings for Advent; one for Christmas; three for Lent; two for Easter, six for Ordinary Time, and one Miscellaneous set for fifty-two continuous or semi-continuous days. Also, there are alternative biblical passages presented for the solemnities that occur throughout the liturgical year. Overall, the goal is to present possibilities to read (hear) more of the Bible over the course of many years than what is currently read (heard) over three years.

These alternative First Reading proposals consist of biblical pericopes arranged in a semi-continuous order. It must be noted that only biblical material not found in the Lectionary is presented in the alternative First Readings. If a passage from a biblical book is found in the Lectionary, then it is omitted in the semi-continuous alternatives. Any reader using the alternatives for Bible study and not recalling a passage from the Lectionary, may desire to read the verses omitted from the alternative in order to preserve the sequence, sense, and context of the pericopes. For the benefit of the reader, after the biblical notation is given in the alternative a word

6. Schuller, "Bible," 1769.
7. Schuller, "Bible," 1770.

or a few words in parentheses follows, indicating the subject of the passage; when a subject appears several times—such as David 1, David 2, David 3—the number indicates that a long pericope has been divided into more than one section.

Recommendation

In order to see what has been included in the Lectionary from the Bible and/or what has been left out of the Bible, this author recommends highlighting a New American Bible or a New American Bible Revised Edition using the notations found in chapter 3. Use either the biblical notations indicating what is in the Lectionary from the Bible (bold) or what is in the Bible but not in the Lectionary (italics). Once the highlighting is completed, flip through the pages and notice the highlighted passages as compared to the material not highlighted.

Notes on the Bible

Three Sections

The Bible is divided into two parts: The Hebrew Bible (Old Testament) and the Christian Bible (New Testament). The Hebrew Bible consists of thirty-nine named books accepted by Jews and Protestants as Holy Scripture. The Old Testament also contains those thirty-nine books plus seven to fifteen more named books or parts of books called the Apocrypha or the Deuterocanonical Books; the Old Testament is accepted by Catholics and several other Christian denominations as Holy Scripture. The Christian Bible, consisting of twenty-seven named books, is also called the New Testament; it is accepted by Christians as Holy Scripture. Thus, in this work:

—**Hebrew Bible (Old Testament)**, abbreviated **HB (OT)**, indicates that a book is found both in the Hebrew Bible and the Old Testament;

—**Old Testament** (**Apocrypha**), abbreviated **OT** (**A**), indicates that a book (or a part of a book) is found only in the Old Testament Apocrypha and not in the Hebrew Bible;

—and **Christian Bible** (**New Testament**), abbreviated **CB** (**NT**), indicates that a book is found only in the Christian Bible or New Testament.

In notating biblical texts, the first number refers to the chapter in the book, and the second number (following the colon) refers to the verse within the chapter. Thus, HB (OT) Isa 7:11 means that the quotation comes from Isaiah, chapter 7, verse 11. OT (A) Sir 39:30 means that the quotation comes from Sirach, chapter 39, verse 30. CB (NT) Mark 6:2 means that the quotation comes from Mark's Gospel, chapter 6, verse 2. When more than one sentence appears in a verse, the letters a, b, c, etc. indicate the sentence being referenced in the verse. Thus, HB (OT) 2 Kgs 1:6a means that the quotation comes from the Second Book of Kings, chapter 1, verse 6, sentence 1. Also, poetry, such as the Psalms and sections of Judith, Proverbs, and Isaiah, may be noted using the letters a, b, c, etc. to indicate the lines being used. Thus, Ps 16:4a refers to the first line of verse 4 of Psalm 16; there are two more lines of verse 4: b and c.

Because there may be a difference in the verse numbers between any Bible not The New American Bible (NAB) or The New American Bible Revised Edition (NABRE), this author recommends the use of the Catholic Bible upon which the Lectionary is based: NAB or NABRE. It is also important to note that in some books verse numbering is not in consecutive order; modern biblical scholarship has corrected verse numbering. Thus, verse 12 may be followed by verse 6, indicating that the current placement of the verse is out of sequence. Verse 6 belongs after verse 5 and before verse 7, even though in older Bibles it followed verse 12!

In the HB (OT) and the OT (A), the reader often sees LORD (note all capital letters). Because God's name (Yahweh or YHWH, referred to as the Tetragrammaton) is not to be pronounced, the name Adonai (meaning *Lord*) is substituted for Yahweh when a biblical text is read. When a biblical text is translated and printed, LORD (Gen 2:4) is used to alert the reader to what the text states: Yahweh. Furthermore, when the biblical author writes Lord Yahweh, printers present Lord GOD (note all capital letters for GOD; Gen 15:2) to avoid the printed ambiguity of LORD LORD. When the reference is to Jesus, the word printed is Lord (note capital L and lower-case letters; Luke 11:1). When writing about a lord (note all lower-case letters; Matt 18:25) with servants, no capital L is used.

Bibles

Most Bible readers are not aware that there is no such thing as the original Bible! The fact is: There are Bibles. First, there is the Jewish Bible, often called the Hebrew Bible; its books were collected and completed between 70 and 90 CE based on the Jerusalem canon (collection) in this order: Torah (Genesis, Exodus, Leviticus, Numbers, Deuteronomy), Prophets (Isaiah, Jeremiah, Ezekiel, etc.), and Writings (Job, Psalms, Proverbs, etc.). It is important to note the arrangement of the collected books. Second, there is—for want of a better name—the Christian Hebrew Bible or the Christian Old Testament, completed in the fourth century CE, but not defined until after the Reformation. It consists of Torah, Writings, and Prophets. It is important to note the (re)ordering of the collected books. Christianity took the Jewish (Hebrew) Bible and rearranged the order of its books into what is known among Christians as the Christian Hebrew Bible or the Christian Old Testament!

The Jerusalem canon, obviously, is the collection of biblical books used in Jerusalem and its environs. A large community of Jews, however, lived in Alexandria, Egypt. To the Jerusalem canon (books in Hebrew and Aramaic) they added books in Greek, the language they spoke; this collection is the Alexandrine canon (collection). They also translated the Jerusalem canon's books from Hebrew and Aramaic into Greek. That translation, containing books and parts of books not in the Jerusalem canon, is called the Septuagint (abbreviated LXX). Later, the Septuagint was translated into Latin; it is known as the Vulgate. Every time a book of the Bible is translated, it picks up something and it loses something; that is because there is no such thing as literary equivalence. Furthermore, translators' biases (such as language knowledge, vocabulary, personal beliefs, presuppositions, etc.) affect the translation.

Thus, we have (1) the Hebrew Bible—the Jewish Bible, (2) the Hebrew Bible (Old Testament)—the rearranged books of the Hebrew Bible, and (3) the Christian Bible—twenty-seven books originally written in Greek. The Protestant Bible contains only the books in the Jerusalem canon, but rearranged into the Old Testament, plus the Christian Bible books; the Catholic Bible contains the books in the Alexandrine collection plus the Christian Bible books.

The extra books or parts of books found in the Catholic Bible (and coming from the Alexandrine collection of the Jewish Bible), but not found in a Protestant Bible, are collectively referred to as the Apocrypha or Deuterocanonical Books. They include Tobit, Judith, additions to Esther, Wisdom (of Solomon), Sirach (Ecclesiasticus), Baruch, Letter of Jeremiah (addition to Baruch), Prayer of Azariah (addition to Daniel), Susanna (addition to Daniel), Bel and the Dragon (addition to Daniel), 1 Maccabees, 2 Maccabees, 1 Esdras, Prayer of Manasseh, Psalm 151, 3 Maccabees, 2 Esdras, and 4 Maccabees. Not every Christian group, such as Catholics, accepts all the books in the Apocrypha as Scripture; for example, out of the four books of Maccabees, Catholics accept only 1 and 2 Maccabees. In Catholic Bibles, the additional books are placed with similar books. Thus, First and Second Maccabees are inserted with the historical books; the books of Wisdom and Sirach are found in the wisdom literature section.

Thus, there is no single or original Bible; there are many Bibles; it depends on what books a specific denomination or group (Jews, Christians) accepts as Scripture. The Bible that contains any book that any group accepts as Scripture is *The Access Bible* (updated edition): *New Revised Standard Version with the Apocrypha*, general editors Gail R. O'Day and David Petersen, published in New York by Oxford University Press in 1999 and updated in 2011. *The Access*

Bible presents the Old Testament books, the Apocryphal/Deutero-canonical Books, then the New Testament books.

Thus, a Bible reader should keep in mind the following: In a Christian Bible, The Old Testament consists of the rearranged books found in the Hebrew (Jewish) Bible. Roman Catholics and some others add some books and parts of books to that Old Testament because they were found in the Alexandrine collection. In general, Protestants do not add books to the Old Testament; they follow the Jerusalem collection of books, but rearrange them as noted above. Almost all Christians accept the twenty-seven books of the New Testament; there are a few groups that reject one or another of the books in the collection.

Presuppositions

The HB (OT) begins as stories passed on by word of mouth from one person to another. Sometime during the oral transmission stage, authors decided to collect the oral stories and write them. A change occurs immediately. One does not tell a story the same way one writes a story. Repetition and correction occur in oral story-telling. Except for future emendations by copyists, single statements by characters and plot structure dominate written stories. Furthermore, in both oral and written story-telling, types or models are employed. In the HB (OT), for example, Joshua and Elijah are types of Moses. In the CB (NT) Elizabeth becomes a type of Hannah, who is herself a type of Sarah. When orally narrating or writing a story, the teller or author consciously creates one character as a type of another in order to make the character and his or her words and actions intelligible to the reader (hearer).

In the CB (NT) the oldest gospel is Mark's account of Jesus' victory. The author of Matthew's Gospel copied and shortened about eighty percent of Mark's material into his book and then added other stories to make the work longer. The author of Luke's Gospel copied and shortened about fifty percent of Mark's material into his orderly account and then added other stories to make the work much longer. The material shared by Matthew and Luke that is not found in Mark's Gospel is called Q—from the German word *Quelle*, meaning *Source*—by biblical scholars. Mark's Gospel begins as oral story-telling, lasting for about forty years in that form. An unidentified author, called Mark for the sake of convenience, collects the oral stories, sets a plot, and writes the first gospel around 70 CE. Because Jesus was expected to return soon, no one had thought about recording what he had said and done until Mark came along and realized that he was not returning as quickly as had been thought. About ten years after Mark finished his gospel, Matthew needed to adopt Mark's narrative—originally intended for a peasant Gentile readership—to a Jewish audience. And about twenty years after Mark finished his gospel, Luke needed to adapt Mark's poor Gentile-intended work for a rich, upper class, urban, Gentile readership. The author of John's Gospel did not know the existence of the other three works collectively named synoptic gospels. Also, the names assigned to gospels do not indicate who the author was; they are used for the sake of convenience to distinguish one gospel from another.

Furthermore, gospels were not first intended to be read privately as is done today. They were meant to be heard in a group. The very low rate of literacy in the first century would have never dictated many copies of texts since most people could not read, and their standard practice was to listen to another read the stories to them. Thus, what began as oral story-telling passed on by word of mouth became written story-telling preserved in gospels. A careful reading of Mark's Gospel will reveal the orality still embedded in the text, especially evident in the repetition of words and the organization of stories in three parts. In rewriting Mark, Matthew and Luke remove the last traces of oral story-telling.

The letters of Paul are older than the gospels. Biblical scholars divide the letters of Paul into the authentic letters—those written by Paul (Romans, Galatians, Philippians, etc.)—and those written by someone else in Paul's name—second generation Pauline letters (Ephesians, Colossians, Titus, etc.). The latter group of letters usually develop Pauline thought for a new generation of Christians. The reader of letters needs to keep in mind that the letter was not addressed to him or her; it was addressed to a specific group of believers in the mid- to late-first century CE. In addition to the Pauline body of letters, there are other letters that were gathered and placed in the CB (NT) canon (collection), such as James, 1 and 2 Peter, Jude, etc. These anonymous letters were written in the name of an apostle to give them authority in the Christian communities to which they were addressed.

1

Analysis[1] of Biblical Book Material in the Lectionary Sunday Cycles A, B, and C and Weekday Years I and II

Hebrew Bible (Old Testament) and Old Testament (Apocrypha)

Genesis: Passages[2] from the book of Genesis are found five times in the Sunday Cycle A year; eight times in the Sunday Cycle B year;

1. This analysis is made from "Appendix II Table of Readings" in *Lectionary for Mass: Volume I*, 1161–73.

2. A passage (lection, pericope) usually consists of six to ten verses printed in sense lines to make easy the public reading (proclamation) of the text. There are passages with fewer verses, and passages with more verses of biblical texts.

and seven times in the Sunday Cycle C year. One passage in the Sunday Cycle is found in all three years.[3] In the Weekday Year I, there are thirty-three passages from Genesis; in Weekday Year II, there are only three passages from Genesis.

Exodus: Passages from the book of Exodus are found seven times in the Sunday Cycle A year; six times in the Sunday Cycle B year; and six times in the Sunday Cycle C year. Two passages in the Sunday Cycle are found in all three years. In the Weekday Year I, there are eighteen passages from Exodus; in Weekday Year II, there are only two passages from Exoduss.

Leviticus: A passage from the book of Leviticus appears in the Sunday Cycles A and B years, but nothing in the Cycle C year. Three passages appear in the Weekday Year I, and one passage in the Weekday Year II.

Numbers: The same passage appears in the Sunday Cycles A, B, and C, and one other passage appears in Sunday Cycle B. Six passages appear in the Weekday Year I, and two, which are repeats from Year I, appear in Weekday Year II.

Deuteronomy: In Sunday Cycle A, there are three passages from Deuteronomy. In Sunday Cycle B, there are five passages, and in Sunday Cycle C there are two passages. Eight passages are found in Weekday Year I, and three in Weekday Year II.

Joshua: One passage from the book of Joshua appears in the Sunday Cycles A and C with no passage in Year B. There are three passages from Joshua in Weekday Year I, but no passages in Weekday Year II.

Judges: No passages from the book of Judges appear in the Sunday Cycles. Five are found in Weekday Year I and one, a repeat from Year I, in Weekday Year II.

---

3. This means that it is repeated annually. For example, the first story of creation is read (heard) yearly during the Easter Vigil, no matter what the Sunday Cycle may be.

Ruth: Like Judges, no passages from the book of Ruth appear in the Sunday Cycles, and only two appear in Weekday Year I.

1 Samuel: One passage from the First Book of Samuel appears in the Sunday Cycles A and B, and two appear in the Sunday Cycle C. There is one passage in Weekday Year I, and twelve in Weekday Year II.

2 Samuel: The Second Book of Samuel is not represented in Sunday Year A, but is found one time in Sunday Year B, and two times in Sunday Year C. One passage—a repeat in Year II— is in Weekday Year I, but eleven are found in Weekday Year II.

1 Kings: Both Sunday Cycles A and B have two passages from the First Book of Kings, while Sunday Cycle C has three. No passages are read in Weekday Year I, but six are read in Weekday Year II.

2 Kings: There is one passage from the Second Book of Kings in Sunday Cycles A, B, and C. Two passages—both repeated in Year II—are found in Weekday Year I, and nine in Weekday Year II.

1 Chronicles: No passages are read from the book of First Chronicles in Sunday Cycles or in Weekdays.

2 Chronicles: One passage from Second Chronicles is read in Sunday Cycle B, but none are read in Sunday Cycles A or C. Three passages are read in Weekday Year I, and one in Weekday Year II.

Ezra: No passages are read from the book of Ezra in Sunday Cycles or in Weekday Years.

Nehemiah: Only one passage from the book of Nehemiah appears in Sunday Cycle C; no passage from Nehemiah is presented in Sunday Cycle A or B. Two passages appear in Weekday Year I, but none in Weekday Year II.

Tobit: No passages from the OT (A) book of Tobit are read in any Sunday Cycle or Weekday Year II. However, six passages are presented in Weekday Year I.

Judith: No passages are read from the OT (A) book of Judith in any Sunday Cycle or Weekday Year.

Esther: Only one passage from the book of Esther is presented on Weekday I and II, and it is the same passage in both years.

1 Maccabees: No passages from the OT (A) book of First Maccabees are read in any Sunday Cyle or Weekday Year II. In Weekday Year I, four passages are read.

2 Maccabees: Like First Maccabees, no passages are ready in Sunday Cycles A and B nor in Weekday Year II; one passage is read in Sunday Cycle C, and two are read in Weekday Year I.

Job: The book of Job is represented with two passages in Sunday Cycle B. There are no passages in Sunday Cycles A and C nor in Weekday Year I. In Weekday Year II, there are six passages from Job.

Psalms: All one hundred fifty Psalms are represented in the lectionary except for Psalms 11, 14, 20, 35, 38, 39, 53, 58, 64, 70, 73, 75, 76, 83, 108, 120, 125, 129, 133, 134, 140, and 142—for a total of twenty-two.[4]

Proverbs: In Sunday Cycles A, B, and C, one passage is read from the HB (OT) book of Proverbs. No passages are read in Weekday Year I, and only three in Weekday Year II.

Ecclesiastes: Only one passage from the book of Ecclesiastes in read in Sunday Cycle C. None are read in Sunday Cycles A and B, nor Weekday Year I. Three are read in Weekday Year II.

Song of Songs: The same single passage from the HB (OT) book Song of Songs is read in Weekday Year I and II. No passage is read in Sunday Cycles A, B, or C.

Wisdom: The OT (A) book of Wisdom is represented by two passages in Sunday Cycle A, by three passages in Sunday Cycles B and

---

4. This analysis is made from "Appendix III: Table of Responsorial Psalms and Canticles," in *Lectionary for Mass: Volume I*, 1175–6.

C. Seven selections from Wisdom are presented in Weekday Year I with one—a repeat from Year I—in Weekday Year II.

Sirach: The OT (A) book of Sirach is represented by four passages in Sunday Year A, by two in Sunday Year B, and by five in Sunday Year C. Two of those passages are repeated annually. In Weekday Year I, thirteen passages are assigned, and three in Weekday Year II.

Isaiah: The prophet Isaiah represents the most-quoted HB (OT) book in the Lectionary. There are twenty-six passages in Sunday Cycle A, eighteen in Sunday Cycle B, and sixteen in Sunday Cycle C. Twelve passages are repeated annually. In Weekday Year I, there are twenty-six passages, and in Weekday Year II, there are thirty-two passages. Twenty-six of the passages found in Weekday Years I and II are duplicates.

Jeremiah: Passages from the prophet Jeremiah appear twice in Sunday Cycle A, three times in Sunday Cycle B, and four times in Sunday Cycle C. In Weekday Year I, five passages from Jeremiah are presented, and in Weekday Year II, there are twenty, six of which are duplicates from Year I.

Lamentations: Only one passage from the HB (OT) book of Lamentations appears in Weekday Year II. No passages are found in any Sunday Cycle nor in Weekday Year I.

Baruch: The OT (A) book of the prophet Baruch is represented by one passage in Sunday Year A and B, and two in Sunday Cycle C. One passage in Sundays Year A, B, and C is the same pericope. Two passages from Baruch are presented in Weekday Year I, and none in Weekday Year II.

Ezekiel: The HB (OT) prophet Ezekiel is represented by six passages in Sunday Cycle A, four in Sunday Cycle B, and three in Sunday Cycle C; two passages in all three Sunday Cycles are duplicates. Weekday Year I contains three passages, and Weekday Year II contains sixteen passages, three of which are duplicates from Year I.

Daniel: The prophet Daniel is not represented in Sunday Cycles A or C, but two passages appear in Sunday Cycle B. Ten passages from Daniel are found in Weekday Year I, and four—all duplicates of Year I—in Weekday Year II.

Hosea: One passage from the prophet Hosea is found in Sunday Cycle A, two in Sunday Cycle B, and none in Sunday Cycle C. Two passages are found in Weekday Year I, and six in Weekday Year II, two of which are duplicates from Year I.

Joel: The same passage from the prophet Joel is read in Sunday Cycles A, B, and C. Three passages from Joel are found in Weekday Year I, and one—a repeat from Year I—in Weekday Year II.

Amos: The prophet Amos is not represented in Sunday Cycle A nor Weekday Year I, but is found one time in Sunday Cycle B, two times in Sunday Cycle C, and six times in Weekday Year II.

Obadiah: No passages are read from the prophet Obadiah in Sunday Cycles or in Weekday Years.

Jonah: A passage from the book of Jonah is found only in Sunday Cycle B; no passage is found in Sunday Cycles A or C. Four passages are found in Weekday Year I, and one in Weekday Year II—which is the same as one in Year I.

Micah: In Sunday Cycle A, no passage from Micah is found; in Sunday Cycle B, no passage from Micah is found; in Sunday Cycle C, one passage from Micah is found. In Weekday Year I, two passages from Micah are found, in Weekday Year II five are found. Two of the five are the same as the two in Year I.

Nahum: The prophet Nahum is represented by one passage in Weekday Year II.

Habakkuk: The prophet Habakkuk is represented by one passage in Sunday Cycle C and one passage in Weekday Year II.

Zephaniah: The prophet Zephaniah is represented by one passage in Sunday Cycles A and C, and the same two passages in Weekday Years I and II.

Haggai: The prophet Haggai is represented by two passages in Weekday Year I.

Zechariah: One passage from Zechariah is read in Sunday Cycle A, none in Sunday Cycle B, and one in Sunday Cycle C. Three passages are read in Weekday Year I. No passages are read in Weekday Year II.

Malachi: The prophet Malachi is represented with one passage in Sunday Cycles A and C, two passages in Weekday Year I, and one passage, a duplicate from Year I, in Weekday Year II.

Christian Bible (New Testament)

Matthew: Passages from Matthew's Gospel are read exclusively in Sunday Cycle A, and in Weekdays I and II, Ordinary Time weeks ten through 21. There are passages from Matthew's Gospel that are never read.[5]

Mark: Passages from Mark's Gospel are read exclusively in Sunday Cycle B, and in Weekday I and II, Ordinary Time weeks one through nine. There are passages from Mark's Gospel that are never read.

Luke: Passages from Luke's Gospel are read exclusively in Sunday Cycle C, and in Weekday I and II, Ordinary Time weeks twenty-two through thirty-four. There are passages from Luke's Gospel that are never read.

John: In Sunday Cycle A, nineteen passages are read from John's Gospel. In Sunday Cycle B, twenty-eight passages are read from John's Gospel. In Sunday Cycle C, twenty passage are read from

5. See chapter 3 for a list of passages read (heard) and not read (heard) from the Gospels according to Mark, Matthew, Luke, and John.

John's Gospel. Eleven of the passages in all three cycles are duplicates. In Weekday Years I and II, 65 duplicate passages are read from John's Gospel.

Acts of the Apostles: Because the Acts is read during the Easter Season, eleven passages are found in Sunday Cycles A, B, and C, and five of those are duplicates. The same forty-two passages are read in Weekdays Year I and II.

Romans: Paul's Letter to the Romans is represented by twenty-four passages in Sunday Cycle A, by five in Sunday Cycle B, and by six in Sunday Cycle C; two are duplicate passages read (heard) annually. Twenty-four passages are read in Weekday Year I, and none in Year II.

1 Corinthians: Paul's First Letter to the Corinthians is represented by twelve passages in Sunday Cycle A, ten in Sunday Cycle B, and twelve in Sunday Cycle C. Three passages are read annually. No passages are found in Weekday Year I, but twenty-one passages are found in Weekday Year II.

2 Corinthians: Paul's Second Letter to the Corinthians is represented by one passage in Sunday Cycles A and C, but eight in Sunday Cycle B. Weekday Year I presents thirteen passages from the Second Letter to the Corinthians, but Weekday Year II has but one, a duplicate of one in Year I.

Galatians: Paul's Letter to the Galatians is represented by one passage in Sunday Cycle A, by two in Sunday Cycle B, and by seven in Sunday Cycle C. There is one passage that is the same in all three Sunday Cycle. No passages are read in Weekday Year I, but nine are read in Weekday Year II.

Ephesians: Passages from the second-generation Pauline Letter to the Ephesians are found four times in Sunday Cycle A, thirteen times in Sunday Cycle B, and three times in Sunday Cycle C; three of those passages are duplicates. In Weekday Year I, there are no passages from Ephesians, but in Weekday Year II, there are thirteen passages.

Philippians: From Paul's Letter to the Philippians, there are five passages in Sunday Cycles A and C, and one passage in Sunday Cycle B; one passage occurs in all three cycles. No passages occur in Weekday Year I, but eight occur in Weekday Year II.

Colossians: Passages from the second-generation Pauline Letter to the Colossians are found two times in Sunday Cycles A and B and seven times in Sunday Cycle C; two of those passages are duplicates. In Weekday Year I, there are eight passages from Colossians, but in Weekday Year II, there are no passages.

1 Thessalonians: Paul's First Letter to the Thessalonians is represented by five passages in Sunday Year A, and by one in Sunday, Cycles B and C. Eight passages occur in Weekday Year I, but no passages in Year II.

2 Thessalonians: No passages from the second-generation Pauline Second Letter to the Thessalonians occur in either Sunday Cycle A or B, but three appear in Sunday Cycle C. No passages are found in Weekday Year I, but three are found in Year II.

1 Timothy: No passages from the second-generation Pauline First Letter to Timothy are found in Sunday Cycles A or B, but three occur in Sunday Cycle C. Eight passages represent First Timothy in Weekday Year I, but none in Year II.

2 Timothy: In Sunday Cycle A, one passage represents the second-generation Pauline Second Letter to Timothy, while none are found in Sunday Cycle B but four in Sunday Cycle C. No passages from Second Timothy are found in Weekday Year I, but four are found in Weekday Year II.

Titus: In the second-generation Pauline Letter to Titus, two passages are found in Sunday Cycles A and B, and three are found in Sunday Cycle C; two of the passages are duplicates in Cycles A, B, and C. In Weekday Year I, there are no representative passages, and in Weekday Year II, there are three.

Philemon: In Paul's Letter to Philemon, there is only one passage in Sunday Cycle C and one in weekday Year II.

Hebrews: In Sunday Cycle A, there are two passages from Hebrews. In Sunday Cycle B, there are twelve passages. In Sunday Cycle C, there are eight passages. There are two duplicate passages read (heard) in Sunday Cycles A, B, and C. While there are twenty-five passages in Weekday Year I, there are no passages in Year II.

James: The Letter of James is represented in Sunday Cycle A by one passage, in Sunday Cycle B by five passages, and by no passages in Sunday Cycle C or in Weekday Year I. There are twelve passages in Weekday Year II.

1 Peter: The First Letter of Peter is represented by six passages in Sunday Cycle A, by one in Sunday Cycle B, and by no passages in Sunday Cycle C nor Weekday Year I. There are five passages from First Peter in Weekday Year II.

2 Peter: A total of three passages represent the Second Letter of Peter. One is found in Sunday Cycle B, and two are found in Weekday Year II.

1 John: In Sunday Cycle A, the First Letter of John is represented by two passages. In Sunday Cycle B, the First Letter of John is represented by six passages. In Sunday Cycle C, no passages represent the First Letter of John. While there are fourteen passages in Weekday Year I and II, all fourteen of them are duplicates.

2 John: The Second Letter of John is represented by one passage in Weekday Year II.

3 John: The Third Letter of John is represented by one passage in Weekday Year II.

Jude: The Letter of Jude is represented by one passage in Weekday Year II.

Revelation: No passages represent the book of Revelation in Sunday Cycle A. One passage represents the book of Revelation in Sunday Cycle B. Six passages represent the book of Revelation in Sunday Cycle C. One passage is found in Weekday Year I—a duplicate of one in Year II—and thirteen are found in Weekday Year II.

Conclusions

Those attending only Sunday never hear passages from Judges, Ruth, Tobit, Esther, 1 Maccabees, Lamentations, Song of Songs, Haggai, 2 John, 3 John, and Jude.

In the Sunday Cycles only one passage is read from Leviticus (in Cycles A and B), Joshua (in Cycles A and C), 1 Samuel (in Cycles A and B) 2 Samuel (in Cycle B), 2 Kings (in Cycles A, B, and C), 2 Chronicles (in Cycle B), Nehemiah (in Cycle C), 2 Maccabees (in Cycle C), Proverbs (in Cycles A, B, and C), Ecclesiastes (in Cycle C), Baruch (in Cycles A and B), Joel (in Cycles A, B, and C), Amos (in Cycle B), Jonah (in Cycle B), Micah (in Cycle C), Habakkuk (in Cycle C), Zephaniah (in Cycles A and C), Malachi (in Cycles A and C), 2 Corinthians (in Cycles A and C), Galatians (in Cycle A), Philippians (in Cycle B), 1 Thessalonians (in Cycles B and C) 2 Timothy (in Cycle A), Philemon (in Cycle C), James (in Cycle A), 1 Peter (in Cycle B), and Revelation (in Cycle B). The reading of one passage during a whole year does not represent the contents of a biblical book!

In the Weekday Year I and II, there is only one passage read from the following books: Judges (in Year II), 1 Samuel (in Year I), 2 Samuel (in Year I), 2 Chronicles (in Year II), Esther (in Year I and II, same passage), Wisdom (in Year II), Lamentations (in Year II), Joel (in Year II), Jonah (in Year II), Nahum (in Year II), Habakkuk (in Year II), Malachi (in Year II), 2 Corinthians (in Year II), Philemon (in Year I), 2 John (in Year II), 3 John (in Year II), Jude (in Year II), and Revelation (in Year I).

In the Weekday Years I and II, no passage is read from the following books: Ruth (in Year II), 1 Kings (in Year I), Nehemiah (in Year II), Tobit (in Year II), 1 Maccabees (in Year II), Job (in Year I), Proverbs (in Year I), Ecclesiastes (in Year I), Lamentations (in Year I), Baruch (in Year II), Amos (in Year I), Nahum (in Year I), Habakkuk (in Year I), Haggai (in Year II), Zechariah (in Year II), Galatians (in Year I), Ephesians (in Year I), Philippians (in Year I), Colossians (Year II), 1 Thessalonians (in Year II), 2 Thessalonians (in Year I), 1 Timothy (in Year II), 2 Timothy (in Year I), Titus (in Year I), Philemon (in Year I), Hebrews (in Year II), James (in Year I), 1 Peter (in Year I), 2 Peter (in Year I), 2 John (in Year I), 3 John (in Year I), and Jude (in Year I).

There is a heavy concentration—meaning over twenty passages—from the following books: Genesis (55 passages), Exodus (39 passages), Deuteronomy (21 passages), Sirach (27 passages), Isaiah (108 passages), (Jeremiah (34 passages), Ezekiel (32 passages), Acts (75 passages), Romans (59 passages), 1 Corinthians (55 passages), 2 Corinthians (24 passages), Ephesians (33 passages), Hebrews (47 passages), and Revelation (21 passages).

All of the Gospels of Matthew (Year A), Mark (Year B), and Luke (Year C) are read over three years, and every year Mark, Matthew, and Luke are read in both Weekdays Year I and II. See the next chapter for passages not ever read from the Synoptic Gospels (Mark, Matthew, Luke).

No biblical passages are ever heard or read from 1 Chronicles, Ezra, Judith, or Obadiah.

The Lectionary does not contain the whole Bible. The Lectionary is a Bible within a Bible; it has been created from the Roman Catholic Bible, and it has given more authority to some books by the number of passages read from them, and it has given less authority to some books by the one or few passages read from them; and it has given no authority to the four books from which no passages are taken.

Any type of Bible Study that is based on the Lectionary is not Bible Study; it is Lectionary Study. For example, Mahri Leonard-Fleckman's *Ponder: Contemplative Bible Study* for Years A, B, and C—part of the Little Rock Scripture Study Program—is not Bible Study; it is Lectionary Study. Lectionary Study focuses on a text (passage, pericope) out of its context (whole book and whole Bible) and violates the prescription found in the "Dogmatic Constitution on Divine Revelation" of Vatican Council II (pars 11–12). Furthermore, because the HB (OT) First Reading in the Sunday Cycles was chosen by the Lectionary committee to echo something in the Gospel passage, a new context has been given to both the First Reading and the Gospel. Inserted between them is the Second Reading, a semi-continuous reading from a CB (NT) letter, which loses its context as a section of a whole letter and can contribute to the recontexting of the HB (OT) passage and Gospel passage. The context and recontexting question is not as severe on Weekdays I and II because both the First Reading and the Gospel (there is no Second Reding on Weekdays) are semi-continuous and not connected.

The *Lectionary* and the *Bible*

2

Analysis: What Is not Read (Heard) from the Bible in the Lectionary Sunday Cycles or Weekday Years

Hebrew Bible (Old Testament) and Old Testament (Apocrypha)

Genesis

2:10–14 (River in Eden with four branches)

4:16–24 (Cain's descendants)

4:26—5:7, 9–32 (From Adam to Noah)

6:1–4 (The Nephilim)

6:9–22 (Preparations for the Great Flood)

7:6–9 (Entering the Ark)

7:11—8:5 (The Great Flood)

8:14–19 (Leaving the Ark)

9:16–28 (Covenant, Noah's descendants)

10:1–32 (More Noah's descendants)

11:10–26 (From Shem to Abram)

11:27–32 (Terah's descendants)

12:10—13:1 (Abram and Sarai in Egypt)

13:3–4 (Abram travels to Bethel)

14:1–17, 21–24 (Abram and four kings)

15:13–16 (Prediction concerning Abram's descendants)

15:19–21 (Land owners)

16:13–14 (Hagar speaks to the LORD's messenger)

17:11–14 (Covenant mark: circumcision)

17:23–27 (Abraham circumcises all males in his household)

19:1–14 (Sodom and Gomorrah destroyed)

19:30–38 (Lot and his two daughters)

20:1–18 (Abraham, Sarah, and Abimelech)

21:4 (Abraham circumcises Isaac)

21:6–7 (Sarah laughs after Isaac's birth)

21:22–34 (Abraham and Abimelech seal a pact)

22:20–24 (Abraham's brother's sons)

23:5–18, 20 (Abraham buys the cave of Machpelah
    for a family burial site)

24:9–47, 52–57 (Abraham's servant finds a wife for Isaac)

25:1–18 (Abraham's second marriage and death;
    Ishmael's descendants)

25:19–34 (Birth of Esau and Jacob to Isaac)

26:1–35 (Isaac and Abimelech)

27:6–14, 30–46 (Rebekah helps Jacob deceive Isaac)

28:1–9 (Jacob and Esau get wives)

29:1—32:21 (Jacob works for Laban, marries Leah and Rachel,
    leaves Laban)

33:1–20 (Esau meets Jacob)

34:1–31 (Jacob's daughter, Dinah, raped, revenged)

35:5, 8–29 (Jacob, God, and Jacob's sons)

36:1–43 (Esau's descendants)

37:1–2, 5–11, 13b–17a, 29–36 (Joseph, the dreamer,
    sold by his brothers)

38:1–29 (Judah, Er, Onan, Tamar)

39:1–23 (Potiphar purchases Joseph; Potiphar's wife attempts
    to seduce Joseph)

40:1—41:54 (Joseph interprets dreams; Joseph put in charge
    of Egypt's food supply, married)

42:1–4, 7b–16, 24b—44:17, 22, 30–34; 45:6–28 (Joseph and
    his brothers in Egypt)

46:8–27, 31–33; 47:1–31 (Israel's migration to Egypt;
    settlement in Goshen)

48:1—49:7, 11–28, 33 (Jacob [Israel] blesses Joseph's sons;
    Jacob's farewell and death)

50:1–14, 26 (Jacob's burial; Joseph's death)

Exodus

1:1–7 (Jacob's prolific descendants in Egypt)

1:15–20 (Midwives instructed to kill baby Hebrew boys)

2:15b–24 (Moses in Midian)

3:21–22 (God favors the Hebrews over the Egyptians)

4:1–31 (Moses' mission from God; Aaron appointed assistant;
    Moses returns to Egypt)

5:1—11:9a (Moses, Aaron, and Pharaoh; plagues)

12:15–20 (Unleavened bread directions)

12:28–36 (Death of firstborn, Hebrews prepare to leave Egypt)

12:43–51 (Regulations concerning Passover)

13:1—14:4 (Consecration of first-born; journey to Red Sea)

15:18–27 (Miriam with tambourine dances and sings;
    fresh water)

16:6–8 (Grumbling Israelites)

16:16–35 (Manna)

17:14–15 (Amalek not remembered)

18:1–27 (Moses and his father-in-law Jethro)

19:12, 21–25 (Regulations for Israelites at Mount Sinai)

20:18—22:19, 27—23:19, 24–24:2 (Laws)

24:9–18 (Moses on Sinai [Horeb] mountain for forty days)

25:1—31:18 (The ark, tent, and its furnishings)

32:1-6, 25-29, 35 (Golden calf)

33:1-6 (God not traveling with Israelites)

33:12—34:3 (Moses convinces God to travel with Israelites; renewal of the covenant tablets)

34:10-27; 35:1—40:15, 22-33 (Laws, construction of ark, altar, tent)

Leviticus

1:1—7:38 (Holocausts and offerings)

8:1—9:24 (Ordination of Aaron and his sons)

10:1-20 (Priestly conduct)

11:1—12:8; 13:3-43, 47—16:34 (Cleanness and uncleanness)

17:1—18:30; 19:3-10, 19—23:3, 12-14, 17-25, 28-32, 38-44 (Maintaining holiness)

24:1-23 (Sanctuary light, showbread, blasphemy)

25:1-7, 18-55 (Sabbatical year)

26:1—27:34 (Obedience and disobedience, redeeming offerings)

Numbers

1:1—3:4, 10—4:49 (Census, tribes, Aaron's sons)

5:1—6:21 (Laws, Nazirites)

7:1-89 (Twelve days of offerings)

8:1-26 (Levites)

9:1—11:4a (Passover, trumpets, Israel on the move)

11:18-23, 31-35 (Quail)

12:13–16 (Miriam's leprosy)

13:3–24 (Scouts sent to reconnoiter Canaan)

14:2–25, 30–33, 36–45 (Grumbling, Caleb)

15:1–41 (Offerings)

16:1–35 (Korah, Dathan, and Abiram)

17:1—19:22 (Priestly duties)

20:14–29 (King of Edom, Aaron's death)

21:1–3 (Battle)

21:10—22:1 (Journey and Battles)

22:2—24:1, 8–14, 17c–25 (Balak and Balaam)

25:1–18 (Baal worship, Phinehas)

26:1–65 (Census)

27:1–23 (Zelophehad's daughters, Joshua—Moses' successor)

28:1—29:39 (Sacrifices)

30:1–17 (Vows)

31:1–54 (Midianites exterminated)

32:1–42 (Gad and Reuben)

33:1—36:13 (Summary: Stages of the journey from Egypt to
    Promised Land)

Deuteronomy

1:1–8, 15—3:29 (Moses' summary of journey from Egypt
    to Promised Land)

4:3–4, 10–31, 41–43 (Idolatry and fidelity)

4:44—5:11, 16–32 (Covenant terms)

6:14—7:5 (Commandments)

7:12—8:1 (Blessings of obedience)

8:4–6, 19—10:7, 10–11 (God's discipline, gift of land, golden calf, tablets)

11:1–17, 19–25, 29–31 (God's gifts)

12:1—18:14, 21–22 (Statutes and decrees)

19:1—24:16; 25:1—26:3, 11–15 (More statutes and decrees)

27:1—28:69 (Curses and blessings)

29:1–28; 30:5–9 (God's favors)

31:9–30 (Reading of the law, Joshua commissioned)

32:44—33:29 (Blessing the tribes)

Joshua

1:1–18 (The LORD addresses Joshua)

2:1–24 (Rahab saves Israelite spies)

3:1–6, 10b, 12 (Preparing to cross the Jordan River)

4:1–24 (Memorial stones in Jordan River, crossing Jordan River)

5:1–8 (Circumcision of the men)

5: 13—6:27 (Jericho)

7:1—8:28 (Ai)

9:1—10:43 (Gibeon)

11:1—12:24 (Conquered lands and kings)

13:1—19:51 (Division of the land by tribe)

20:1–9 (Asylum cities)

21:1–45 (Cities for Levites and priests)

22:1—23:16 (Some tribes dismissed; Joshua's final words)

24:30–33 (Joshua's death)

Judges

1:1—2:10, 20—3:6 (Israelites conquer the Canaanites, remaining nations)

3:7–31 (Othniel)

4:1—5:31 (Deborah)

6:1–10, 24b—8:35 (Gideon)

9:1–5, 16–57 (Abimelech)

10:1–2 (Tola)

10:3–5 (Jair)

10:6–18 (Ammonite oppression)

11:1–28, 40—12:7 (Jephthah)

12:8–15 (Ibzan, Elon, Abdon)

13:1, 8–23; 14:1—16:31 (Samson)

17:1—19:30 (Micah, the Levite, the Danites, and the concubine)

20:1—21:25 (Israel assembly, war with Benjaminites)

Ruth

1:2, 7–14a, 17–21 (Elimelech, Naomi, Mahlon, Chilion, Orpah, Ruth

2:4–7, 12—4:12, 18–22 Boaz and Ruth)

1 Samuel

1:23, 2:11, 18–21 (Samuel's birth, growth, and dedication)

2:12–17, 22–36 (Death of Eli's sons)

3:11–18, 21b (The LORD appears to Samuel)

4:12–22 (Eli's death, capture of Ark)

5:1—7:17 (The Ark and the Philistines)

8:1–3, 8–9; 9:5–16, 20–27; 10:1b–27 (Request for a king; Saul anointed by Samuel)

11:1—15:15, 24–35: 16:14–23 (Saul, Jonathan, Saul's disobedience, David serves Saul)

17:1–31, 34–36, 38–39, 52–58 (David prepares to meet and defeat Goliath)

18:1–5, 10–30 (David, Jonathan, Saul)

19:8—24:2, 22–23 (Warrior David)

25:1–43 (Samuel's death, Nabal, Abigail, David)

26:1, 3–6, 10–11, 14–21, 24–25 (David spares Saul's life)

27:1–12 (David takes refuge among the Philistines)

28:1–25 (Saul consults the witch of Endor)

29:1—30:31 (David, Philistines, and wars)

31:1–13 (Death of Saul and his sons)

2 Samuel

1:5–10, 13–18, 20–22 (Report of Saul's death)

2:1–11 (David anointed king; Ishbaal anointed king)

2:12—4:12 (War between David and Ishbaal)

5:8–9, 11, 13–16 (David king of all Israel, David's family)

5:17–25 (David and Philistines)

6:1–12a, 16, 20–23, 7:20–23, 25–28 (David brings the Ark
   to Jerusalem)

8:1–18 (David's wars)

9:1–13 (David and Meribaal)

10:1–19 (David, Ammonites, and Arameans)

11:4b, 11–12, 18–27 (David, Bathsheba, and Uriah)

12:7–9, 18–25 (David and Nathan)

12:26–31 (Ammonite war)

13:1–22 (Amnon rapes Tamar)

13:23–15:12 (Absalom)

15:15–29, 31—16:4, 13—18:8, 11–13, 15–23, 25b–29; 19:4–44
   (Absalom)

20:1–25 (Sheba)

21:1–22 (Gibeonites, reburial of Saul and Jonathan)

22:1–51 (David's song)

23:1–38 (David's last words, warriors)

24:1, 3–8, 18–25 (Census)

1 Kings

1:1–53 (King Solomon)

2:5–9, 13—3:3 (David's instructions to Solomon, other matters)

3:15–28 (Solomon's judgment)

4:1—5:14 (Solomon's officers, royal state)

5:15—6:38 (Preparation for and building of the Temple)

7:1–51 (Building of palace, furnishings for the Temple)

8:8, 14–21, 24–26, 31–40, 44–54, 62–66 (Temple dedication, Solomon's prayer)

9:1–28 (God appears to Solomon, acts of King Solomon)

10:11–29 (Solomon's wealth)

11:1–3, 14–25, 33–43 (Solomon's sins and death)

12:1–18, 20–25, 33 (Divided kingdom: Israel and Judah)

13:1–32: (Man of God, Jeroboam, prophet)

14:1–31 (Death of Jeroboam's son, death of Rehoboam of Judah)

15:1–34 (Kings Abijam, Asa, Nadab, Baasha)

16:1–34 (Kings Elah, Zimri, Omri, Ahab)

18:1–19, 40 (Elijah, Obadiah, Ahab, and the prophets of Baal)

19:9b–10, 17–18 (God instructs Elijah)

20:1–42 (King Ahab's victories)

22:1–54 (King Jehoshaphat, Micaiah, King Ahab, King Ahaziah)

2 Kings

1:1–18 (Elijah and King Ahaziah)

2:2–5a, 15–25 (Elijah and Elisha)

3:1–27 (King Joram versus King Mesha)

4:1–7 (Elisha multiplies oil)

4:12–13, 16b–17, 21b–31 (Elisha raises Shunammite's son)

4:38–41 (Elisha fixes poisoned stew)

5:18–27 (Naaman and Gehazi)

6:1—7:20 (Elisha recovers an ax, Aramean soldiers, siege of Samaria)

8:1—9:37 (Prediction of famine, Ben-hadad, Hazael, Jehoram, Ahaziah, anointing of Jehu, death of Ahaziah, death of Jezebel)

10:1–36 (death of Ahab's descendants, destruction of Baal's temple)

11:5–8, 19, 12:1—13:25 (King Joash, death of Elisha)

14:1–29 (King Amaziah)

15:1–38 (Kings Azariah, Zechariah, Shallum, Menahem, Pekahiah, Pekah, Jotham)

16:1—17:4, 9–12, 15b–17, 19–41 (Kings Ahaz, Hoshea, Israel conquered by Assyria)

18:1—19:9a, 12–13, 22–30, 37 (Hezekiah, Sennacherib, Isaiah)

20:7–21 (Hezekiah's illness and death)

21:1—22:7, 14–20; 23:4–30 (Kings Manasseh, Amon, Josiah)

23:31—24:7, 18–20 (Kings Jehoahaz, Jehoiakim, Nebuchadnezzar of Babylon, Zedekiah)

25:13–30 (Destruction of the Jerusalem Temple, Gedaliah appointed governor of Judah)

1 Chronicles

1:1—9:34 (Genealogies by tribe)

9:35—10:14 (Saul)

11:1—14:17 (David)

15:1–2, 5–14, 17–29, 16:3–43 (David brings the Ark to Jerusalem)

17:1–27 (David and Nathan)

18:1—20:8 (David's victories)

21:1–30 (Census)

22:1—29:9, 14–30 (Preparing to build the Temple, David's army, Solomon proclaimed king, David's death)

2 Chronicles

1:1—5:5, 11–12; 6:3—7:22 (King Solomon, building the Temple, dedicating the Temple)

8:1–18 (Solomon's building projects)

9:1–31 (Queen of Sheba, Solomon's wealth, Solomon's death)

10:1–19 (Kingdom divided between Israel and Judah)

11:1—12:16 (Rehoboam)

13:1—16:14 (Abijah, Jeroboam, Asa)

17:1—20:37 (Jehoshaphat)

21:1–20 (Jehoram)

22:1—24:16, 26–27 (Ahaziah, Athaliah, Joash)

25:1–28 (Amaziah)

26:1–23 (Uzziah)

27:1–9 (Jotham)

28:1—32:33 (Ahaz, Hezekiah, Sennacherib's invasion)

33:1–25 (Manasseh, Amon)

34:1—35:26 (Josiah)

36:1–13, 17–18 (Jehoahaz, Jehoiakim, Jehoiachin, Zedekiah)

Ezra

1:7–11 (Jewish exiles return to Jerusalem with wealth)

2:1–70 (Census of returnees)

3:1–13 (Restoration of the altar)

4:1–24 (Samaritan interference with rebuilding the Temple, rebuilding halted)

5:1—6:6, 9–12a, 13–22 (Rebuilding of Temple resumed)

7:1—9:4, 10–15 (The scribe Ezra's deeds: Artaxerxes's decree, returnees, mixed marriages)

10:1–44 (Men of Judah and Benjamin summoned to Jerusalem; foreign wives dismissed)

Nehemiah

1:1–11 (Nehemiah prays for discernment)

2:9–20 (Nehemiah arrives in Jerusalem and takes inventory of what needs to be done to rebuild the city walls)

3:1—4:17 (Workers, opposition)

5:1–19 (Antisocial behavior, Nehemiah's response)

6:1–19 (Plots against Nehemiah)

7:1–72 (Census of returnees)

8:4b, 7, 13–18 (Ezra reads the law, feast of Booths)

9:1—10:40 (Confession of the returnees, recitation of Israelite history)

11:1—12:26 (Jews repopulate Jerusalem)

12:27—13:3 (Rededication of Jerusalem's walls)

13:4–31 (Temple reform, sabbath observance, mixed marriages)

Tobit

1:1–2, 4–22 (Tobit's back story)

3:11b–15, 17b (Sarah's prayer, Raphael's mission)

4:1—5:22 (Tobit sends Tobiah to retrieve money;
   Raphael goes along)

6:1–9, 12–18 (Raphael's instructions to Tobiah)

7:1c–5a; 8:1–3, 10–21 (Tobiah welcomed to Raguel's house;
   demon cast out, wedding feast)

9:1–6 (Tobiah recovers Tobit's money)

10:1—11:4 (Tobiah, Sarah, and Raphael head home to Tobit)

11:14b, 17h–18 (Tobit healed, wedding feast)

12:2–4, 16–19, 22 (Raphael's wages and identify)

13:10–18 (Tobit's prayer)

14:1–15 (Tobit's last words, death, Tobiah's death)

Judith

1:1—7:32 (Jews in peril; Nebuchadnezzar, Holofernes)

8:1, 9—13:17 (Jews delivered by Judith)

14:1—16:25 (Assyrians flee, Judith celebrates)

Esther

A:1—2:23 (Mordecai, Ahasuerus, Vashti, Esther)

3:1—C:11 (Haman's plot against the Jews, Esther's aid,
   Mordecai's prayer)

C:13, 17–22, 26–30 (Esther's prayer)

D:1—5:14 (Esther intercedes with the king for the Jews)

6:1—7:10 (Death of Haman)

8:1—F:10 (Jews saved)

1 Maccabees

1:1–9 (Alexander the Great's rule and death)

1:16–40, 44–53, 58–61 (Persecution of the Jews by Antiochus IV
   Epiphanes)

2:1–14, 30–48, 53–56, 65–70 (Mattathias and sons revolt against
   Antiochus, Mattathias's death)

3:1—4:35, 38–51, 60—5:68 (Judas Maccabeus, Temple purified)

6:14–63 (Death of Antiochus IV, Antiochus's son [Antiochus V]
   succeeds to the throne, campaign against Judas Maccabeus)

7:1–50 (Death of Antiochus V; Demetrius becomes ruler)

8:1–32 (Judas Maccabeus enters a treaty with Rome)

9:1–73 (Demetrius invades Judah, Judas Maccabeus dies,
   Jonathan becomes Jewish leader)

10:1—12:53 (Politics of the empire: Alexander, Demetrius,
   Jonathan, Ptolemy, Trypho)

13:1—16:24 (High Priest Simon, John)

2 Maccabees

1:1—2:18a (Letters to Jews in Egypt)

2:32—3:40 (Heliodorus)

4:1—6:17 (Temple profaned)

7:3–8, 15–19, 32–42 (Martyrdom: Mother and sons)

8:1—9:29 (Judas Maccabeus, Antiochus IV Epiphanes)

10:1–8 (Temple purified)

10:9—12:42; 13:1—15:39 (Exploits of Judas Maccabeus)

Job

1:1—5; 2:1–13 (Introduction to Job)

3:4–10, 18–19, 24–26 (Job's curse)

4:1—5:27 (Eliphaz's first speech)

6:1–30; 7:5 (Job's first reply)

8:1–22 (Bildad's first speech)

9:13, 17—10:22 (Job's second reply)

11:1–20 (Zophar's first speech)

12:1—14:22 (Job's third reply)

15:1–35 (Eliphaz's second speech)

16:1—17:16 (Job's fourth reply)

18:1–21 (Bildad's second speech)

19:1–20, 26–29 (Job's fifth reply)

20:1–29 (Zophar's second speech)

21:1–34 (Job's sixth reply)

22:1–30 (Eliphaz's third speech)

23:1—24:25 (Job's seventh reply)

25:1–6 (Bildad's third speech)

26:1—31:15, 21–23, 26–30, 33–37 (Job's eighth reply)

32:1–37:24 (Elihu's speeches)

38:1–7, 21b—40:2, 6—41:26 (The LORD's speeches to Job)

42:7–11, 17 (Job's restoration and death)

Psalms

11	75
14	76
20	83
35	108
38	120
39	125
53	129
58	133
64	134
70	140
73	142

Proverbs

1:1–33; 2:10—3:26; 4:1–6, 14—8:27, 32–36; 9:7–18
   (Value of Wisdom)

10:1—20:30; 21:7–9, 14—22:16 (First collection:
   Proverbs of Solomon)

22:17—24:34 (Various sayings of the wise)

25:1—29:27 (Second collection: Proverbs of Solomon)

30:1–4 (Words of Agur)

30:10–33 (Numerical Proverbs)

31:1–9, 14–18, 21–29 (Words of Lemuel)

Ecclesiastes

1:1, 12–18, 24–26 (Investigate life)

3:12—6:9 (Vanities)

6:10–12 (Qoheleth's conclusions)

7:1—11:8; 12:9–14 (Sages, epilogue)

Song of Songs

1:1—2:7, 15, 17; 3:4b–11 (What love desires)

4:1—5:1 (The beloved)

5:2—6:12 (Searching for the beloved; finding the beloved)

7:1—8:5, 8–14 (The beauty of love)

Wisdom

1:8–12, 16; 2:1b–11; 3:10—4:6, 16—5:23; 6:17–21 (Justice and its rewards)

6:22—7:6, 11–14, 17–21; 8:2—9:8, 12; 10:1—11:1 (Wisdom is praised)

11:2–21; 12:3–12, 14–15, 20–27; 13:10—18:4, 10–13, 17—19:5, 10–22 (God's providence during the Exodus from Egypt)

Sirach (Ecclesiasticus)

1:11–29; 2:14—3:2, 8–13, 27–29; 4:1–11, 23–31; 5:11—6:4, 18—14:27; 15:7–15; 16:1–28; 17:14–19; 18:1—23:27; 24:8–11, 17–25, 31—25:25; 26:5–15; 27:1–4, 9–30; 28:10—34:26; 35:18–19, 23–24; 36:3–4, 7–12, 20—38:34; 39:2–4, 15—42:14; 43:1–35 (Various moral instructions)

44:2–8, 16—47:1, 14–25; 48:16—50:23, 27–29; 51:28–30 (Praise of Israel's heroes)

Isaiah

1:1–9, 21–31; 2:6—4:1; 5:8–30; 6:9–13 (Israel and Judah indicted)

7:15–25 (Immanuel)

8:1–9, 11–20 (Isaiah's son and disciples)

9:7—10:4, 8–12, 17–34 (The fall of Israel)

11:11–12 (Union of Israel and Judah)

13:1—22:18, 24–25; 23:1–18 (Oracles against other nations)

24:1—25:5, 11–12; 26:10–11, 13–15, 20—27:13 (Apocalypse)

28:1—29:16; 30:1–18, 22, 27—32:14, 19–20; 33:1–24 (The LORD is Israel's and Judah's salvation)

24:1–17 (The LORD avenges Zion)

36:1—37:38, 38:9, 21–22, 39:1–8 (Historical appendix)

40:12–24; 41:1–5, 11–12, 21–29; 42:8—43:15, 23–24, 26–28; 44:6–28; 45:2–3, 9–17, 19–21; 46:1—48:16, 20–22 (Israel's liberation)

49:7, 16—50:3, 9b—52:6, 11–12; 54:15–17 (Israel's sin is healed)

56:3b–5, 9—57:14, 20–21; 59:1–21; 60:7–22; 61:3c–5, 6b–8; 62:6–10; 63:1–6, 10–15, 18–19; 64:1, 8—65:16, 22—66:9, 15–17, 22–24 (The Jews return from Babylon to Jerusalem)

Jeremiah

1:2–3; 2:4–6, 9–11, 14—3:13 18—6:30 (Oracles during the reign of King Josiah)

7:12–22, 29—11:17, 12:1–17; 13:12—14:16; 15:1–9, 11–15; 16:1—17:4, 11–27; 18:7–17, 21—20:6, 14–18 (Oracles during the reign of King Jehoiakim)

21:1—22:30; 23:9—25:38; 26:10, 17–23; 27:1–22; 29:1–32; 30:3–11, 16–17, 23–24; 31:15–30, 38—33:13, 17–26 (Oracles in the last years of Jerusalem)

34:1—38:3, 7, 11—45:5 (Fall of Jerusalem)

46:1—51:64 (Oracles against nations)

52:1–34 (Some history of Jerusalem)

Lamentations

1:1—2:1, 3–9, 15–17, 20–22 (Jerusalem abandoned; the Lord's wrath against Zion)

3:1–16, 27—4:22 (Sufferings of Jeremiah and the people)

5:1–22 (Jeremiah's lament)

Baruch

1:1–14; 2:1—3:8 (Prayer of the exiles)

3:16–31 (Wisdom)

4:13–26 (Jerusalem consoles her children in Babylonian captivity)

4:30–37 (Jerusalem consoled)

6:1–72 (Letter of Jeremiah about idolatry)

Ezekiel

1:1, 6–23; 2:1, 6–7; 3:5–15, 22–27 (Ezekiel called)

4:1:1—8:18; 9:8–9, 24–25; 10:1–17, 23—11:21; 12:13—15:8; 16:16–58; 17:1–21; 18:11–13, 14–20, 29; 19:1—24:14, 25–27 (Siege of Jerusalem and exile of Judahites)

25:1—27:36; 28:11—32:32 (Prophecies against the nations)

33:1–6, 10–33; 34:18—36:15, 17a, 29–38; 38:1—39:29
(Israel saved)

40:1—42:20; 43:7b—46:24; 47:10, 13—48:35 (A new Israel and
a new Temple in Jerusalem)

Daniel

2:1–30, 46–49 (Nebuchadnezzar's dream)

3:1–13, 21–24, 26–33, 44–51, 89–90, 93–94, 96–100 (Nebuchadnezzar's fiery furnace, Azariah's prayer, song of three Jews)

4:1–34 (Nebuchadnezzar's vision of a great tree)

5:7–12, 15, 18–22, 29–30 (Belshazzar sees writing on the wall)

6:1–11, 29 (Daniel in the lion's den)

7:1, 28—9:3, 11—11:45; 12:4–13 (Daniel's visions)

13:10–14, 31–32, 63–64 (Susanna)

14:1–42 (Bel and the Dragon)

Hosea

1:1—2:15, 17, 19–20, 23—3:5 (Hosea's marriage and children)

4:1–15; 6:7–11; 7:1—8:3, 8–10, 14—9:17; 10:4–6, 9–11, 13–15;
11:5–8, 10—14:1 (Israel's crimes, guilt, punishment)

Joel

1:1–12, 16–20 (Israel invaded by locusts)

2:3–11, 19–20, 25 (The day of the Lord)

4:1–11 (Judgment of the nations)

Amos

1:1—2:5, 11–12 (Judgment of the nations)

3:9—4:10, 13—5:3, 5–13, 16–20, 25–27, 6:1b–3, 8–14 (Words and woes)

7:1–9; 8:1–3, 7–8, 13–14; 9:1–10 (Visions)

Obadiah

1:1–21 (Edom shall perish, the cause, judgment of nations, Judah restored)

Jonah

(all of Jonah is read[heard])

Micah

1:1–16 (God's judgment)

2:6—3:12 (Social evils, downfall of leaders)

4:5–14; 5:4b–14 (Restoration)

6:5, 9—7:6, 10–13, 16–17 (Accusation, condemnations, prayer)

Nahum

1:1–14; 2:2–14; 3:4–5, 8–19 (God's judgment of Nineveh)

Habakkuk

1:1, 4–11; 2:5–20 (Habakkuk complains to God, who answers)

3:1–19 (Habakkuk's canticle/prayer)

Zephaniah

1:1—2:2, 14–15 (The day of the Lord)

3:3–8 (Reproach and promise for Jerusalem)

Haggai

1:9–14; 2:10–23 (Rebuilding the Temple)

Zechariah

1:1—2:4, 10–11 (Four horsemen, horns, blacksmiths)

3:1—5:11 (Joshua the High Priest, flying scroll and bushel)

6:1—7:14 (Four chariots, coronation, fasting)

8:9–19; 9:1–8, 11—10:12 (The Lord and new things)

11:1—12:9, 12–14; 13:2–5, 8—14:21 (Jerusalem restored)

Malachi

1:1–14a; 2:2b–7, 11–17 (Sins of priests, Levites, and people)

3:5–12, 20b–22 (Messenger of the covenant)

Christian Bible (New Testament)

Matthew

4:18–22 (Call of the first disciples)

12:9–13, 22–37, 43–45 (Man with a withered hand, Jesus and Beelzebul, tree and fruits, unclean spirit)

15:3–9, 15–20 (Traditions, parable explained)

15:38—16:12 (Feeding, demand for a sign)

18:6–9 (Temptation)

20:29–33 (Healing two blind men)

21:12–22 (Cleansing of the Temple, cursing the fig tree)

22:22–33, 41–45 (Questions about resurrection and David's son)

23:33—24:3 (Denunciation of scribes and Pharisees, lament over Jerusalem, destruction of Temple)

24:15–36 (Great tribulation, coming of Son of Man)

26:1–13 (Conspiracy and anointing)

Mark

13:1–23 (Destruction of Temple, great tribulation)

16:8b (The shorter ending)

Luke

1:80 (Summary statement about John the Baptist)

3:19–20 (John the Baptist put in prison by Herod)

3:29–38 (Jesus' ancestors)

8:21–56 (Calming of a storm, healing of Gerasene demoniac, woman with hemorrhage, and Jarius' daughter)

9:10–11a, 27 (Twelve return to Jesus; kingdom coming soon to some)

9:37–43 (Healing a boy with a demon)

11:33–36 (Light, lamp, eye, body)

12:22–31 (Depend on God)

14:34–35 (Salt)

16:16–18 (Sayings about law and divorce)

18:15–34 (Children, rich official, renunciation of riches,
   third prediction of the passion)

20:1–26, 41–47 (Jesus' authority, parable of tenant farmers,
   paying taxes, David's son, denunciation of scribes)

21:37—22:13 (Jesus' teaching in the temple; conspiracy
   against Jesus)

John

2:12 (Off to Capernaum)

4:1–4 (Jesus returns to Galilee via Samaria)

6:70–71 (Jesus calls Judas a devil)

7:3–9, 11–13, 19–24, 31–33 (Jesus at the Feast of Tabernacles)

8:43–50 (Jesus speaks truth to the Jews)

10:19–21 (Jesus' words cause division among the Jews)

11:57 (Pharisees seek to arrest Jesus)

12:17–19 (Jesus' popularity)

12:36b–43 (Unbelief and belief among the Jews)

16:4b (Jesus didn't tell disciples about his departure)

20:30–31 (First conclusion to John's Gospel)

Acts

1:18–19 (Death of Judas)

2:12, 15–21 (Apostles considered drunk)

5:1–11 (Ananias and Sapphira)

7:1–43 (Stephen's speech)

8:9–13, 18–25 (Simon the magician)

9:23–25 (Saul [Paul] in Jerusalem)

10:2–24, 27–32 (Visions of Cornelius and Peter)

12:12–23 (Peter escapes to a house of prayer; Herod's death)

13:5b–12 (Sergius Paulus and Paul)

13:40–42 (Paul's address in a synagogue)

14:1–4 (Paul and Barnabas at Iconium)

15:32–41 (Judas and Silas, Paul and Barnabas)

16:16–21, 35–40 (Paul and Silas imprisoned)

17:1–14, 16–21 (Paul in Thessalonica, Beroea, Athens)

18:19–22; 19:9–40 (Paul in Ephesus, exorcists, silversmiths)

20:1–16 (Journeys, Eutychus)

21:1—22:2, 17–29; 23:1–5 (Paul arrested, imprisoned, defense before the Sanhedrin)

23:12—25:12 (Paul in Caesarea, trial before Felix)

25:22—26:18, 24–32 (Paul's trial before Agrippa)

27:1—28:6, 21–29 (Paul's journey to Rome)

Romans

1:8–15 (Thanksgiving)

1:26–32 (Wickedness)

2:12—3:20, 31 (Law [Torah] and sin)

4:9–12, 14–15 (Faith and righteousness)

5:16b; 6:1 (Grace)

7:1–17, 25b (Freedom from the law [Torah])

9:6—10:7, 19–21 (God's free choice of mercy)

11:2b–10, 13–24 (God has not rejected his people; he has chosen the Gentiles)

12:19—13:7 (Vengeance, obedience to authority)

14:1–6, 13—15:3 (Consider the weak, patience, self-denial)

15:10–13, 22—16:2, 10–15, 17–21 (Paul's plans, need for prayers, commendations)

1 Corinthians

1:14–16 (Those Paul baptized)

3:12–15 (Build on the foundation of Jesus Christ)

4:16–21 (Imitate Paul)

5:9–13 (Purge evil in your midst)

6:12–13a, 15b–16 (Sexual immorality)

7:1–24, 36–40 (Paul's advice to the married)

8:1a, 8–10 (Meat sacrificed to idols)

9:1–15, 20–22a (Paul as an apostle)

10:7–9, 13, 23–30 (Seek the good of others)

11:2–16 (Husbands, wives, and Christ)

11:27–32 (The Lord's supper)

12:1–3a (Unity in diversity)

14:1–40 (Prophecy and speaking in tongues)

15:29–34 (Several practical arguments)

15:38–41, 50 (The resurrected body)

16:1–24 (Collection, travel plans, conclusion)

2 Corinthians

1:8–17, 23—2:17 (Paul's change of plans)

3:12–14 (Hope)

5:2–5, 11–13 (Earthly tent, hope)

6:11—7:16 (Holiness)

8:16—9:5 (Titus, God's gift)

10:1–16; 11:12–17, 19–21a, 31–32; 12:11—13:10 (Paul's ministry)

Galatians

1:3–5 (Greetings)

2:3–6, 15, 17–18 (Faith and Works)

3:15–21; 4:1–3, 9–11, 20–21, 25, 28–30 (God's promises
    to Abraham, Hagar)

5:7–12 (Galatians misled)

6:1–13 (Life in community, conclusion)

Ephesians

1:12 (Praise God's glory)

3:1, 4:18b–19, 25–29 (Guides for life)

6:21–24 (Conclusion)

Philippians

1:12–18b (Proclaiming Christ)

2:19–24; 3:1–2, 15–16; 4:3, 22–23 (Travel plans,
    instructions, conclusion)

Colossians

2:4–5, 16–23 (Firmness of faith)

3:22, 25—4:18 (Slaves and masters)

1 Thessalonians

1:6–8b; 2:14—3:6 (Thessalonians receive the word)

5:7–8, 12–15, 25–28 (Seek what is good)

2 Thessalonians

1:6–11a; 2:3b–13 (God's judgment)

3:13–15 (Do good)

1 Timothy

1:3–11, 18–20 (False doctrine)

2:9–15 (Women)

4:1–11 (Everything created by God is good)

5:1–2, 11—6:2a (Elderly, young widows, presbyters, slaves)

6:20–21 (Warning to Timothy)

2 Timothy

1:15–18; 2:4–7, 16—3:7 (Instructions to Timothy)

3:9, 19–22 (Conclusion)

Titus

1:10–16 (Idle talkers)

2:9–10 (Slaves)

2:15, 3:8–15 (Directives for Titus, Conclusion)

Philemon

1:1–6, 21–25, (Greeting, thanksgiving, conclusion)

Hebrews

1:7—2:4, 13 (The Son higher than angels)

3:1–6, 15–19 (Jesus is superior to Moses)

4:6–10 (Sabbath rest)

5:11—6:9 (Advance in maturity)

7:4–14, 18–24 (Melchizedek and Jesus)

9:1, 4–10, 16–23 (Worship in the first covenant)

10:26–31 (Rejection of the Son of God)

11:20–31 (Faith of Isaac and Moses)

12:12, 16–17, 20, 25–29 (Exhortations)

13:19, 22–25 (Conclusion)

James

2:10–13, 25: 3:11–12 (Keeping the Law [Torah])

4:11–12 (Speak no evil)

1 Peter

1:1–2 Greeting

2:1, 13–19; 3:10–13; 4:1–6; 5:5 (Good Christian behavior)

2 Peter

1:1 (Greeting)

1:8–15, 20–21 (Living virtuously)

2:1–22 (False teaching)

3:1–8a, 16 (Delay of Parousia)

1 John

(all of 1 John is read)

2 John

1:1–3, 10–13 (Greeting and Conclusion)

3 John

1:1–4, 9–15 (Introduction and Conclusion)

Jude

1:1–16, 18–20 (Greetings, false teachers)

Revelation

1:11b, 14–16, 20 (List of churches, description of the Son of man)

2:5–7 (Ephesus' need to repent)

2:12–29 (Letters to Pergamum and Thyatira)

3:7–13 (Letter to Philadelphia)

5:13—7:1 (The Lamb and six seals)

7:5–8 (Those sealed from every tribe)

8:1–2, 5—10:7 (The Lamb and the seventh seal,
   seven trumpets, small scroll)

11:1–3, 13–19 (Measuring rod, heavenly temple)

12:12b—13:18 (Woman, dragon, two beasts)

14:4a, 6–12, 20 (Fall of Babylon)

15:5—16:21 (Plagues)

17:1–18; 18:3–20, 24 (Destruction of Babylon)

19:4, 9b–21(King of kings)

20:5–10 (One thousand years)

21:8; 15–21, 24–27 (Those not admitted to the new Jerusalem,
   as it is described)

22:8–11, 15, 18–19 (Epilogue)

The *Lectionary* and the *Bible*

3

Comparison of Biblical Material in the Roman Catholic Lectionary for Sunday Cycles A, B, C and Weekday Years I and II (**bold**) and Biblical Material not in the Roman Catholic Lectionary (*italics*) with Analytical Conclusions of Biblical Books

Genesis: 1:1—2:9; 2:15–4:15; 4:25; 5:8; 7:1–5, 10; 8:6–13, 20—9:15; 11:1–9; 12:1–9; 13:2, 5–18; 14:18–20; 15:1–12, 17–18; 16:1–12; 17:1–10, 15–22; 18:1–33; 19:15–29; 21:1–5, 8–21; 22:1–19; 23:1–4, 19; 24:1–8, 48–51, 58–67; 27:1–5, 15–29; 28:19–22a; 32:22–33;

35:1–4, 6–7; 37:3–4, 12–13a, 17b–28; 42:5–7b, 17–24a; 44:18–21, 23–29; 45:1–5; 46:1–7, 28–30; 49:8–10, 29–32; 50:15–26a.

Genesis: 4:16–24, 26—5:7, 9—6:4, 9–22; 7:6–9, 11—8:5, 14–19; 9:16—10:32; 11:10–32; 12:10—13:1, 3–4; 14:1–17, 21–24; 15:13–16, 19–21; 16:13–14; 17:11–14, 23–27; 19:1–14, 30—20:18; 21:4, 6–7, 27–34; 22:20–24; 23:5–18; 24:9–47, 52–57; 25:1—26:35; 27:6–14, 30—28:9; 28:22b—32:21; 33:1—34:31; 35:5, 8—37:2; 37:5–11, 13b–17a, 29—42:4, 7c–16, 24b—44:17, 22, 30–34; 45:6–28; 46:8–27, 31—49:7, 11–28, 33—50:14, 26b.

Genesis Conclusion: Besides genealogies, some Noah material, and some Abram/Abraham material, missing from the Lectionary is the destruction of Sodom and Gomorrah, circumcision narratives, patriarchs' concubines giving birth; patriarchs' having multiple wives, the Jacob and Laban story, the Jacob and Esau friction, the rape of Dinah, and most of the story of Joseph in Egypt.

Exodus: 1:8–14, 21—2:15b; 3:1–20; 11:10—12:15, 21–27, 37–42; 14:5–17; 16:1–5, 9–15; 17:1–13; 19:1–11, 13–20; 20:1–17; 22:20–26; 23:20–23; 24:3–8; 32:7–24, 30–34; 33:7–11; 34:4–9, 28–35; 40:17–21, 34–38.

Exodus: 1:1–7, 15–20; 2:15c–24; 3:8, 21–22; 4:1—11:10; 12:15–20, 28–36, 43—14:4; 15:18–27; 16:6–8, 16–36; 17:14—18:27; 19:12, 21–25; 20:18—22:19, 27—23:19, 24—24:2, 9—32:6, 25–29, 35—33:6, 12—34:3, 10–27; 35:1—40:16, 22–33.

Exodus Conclusion: Biblical material missing includes Moses in Midian, Moses' mission, Aaron, all the plagues including the death of the first born, Passover regulations, manna, Jethro, multiple sections of laws except for the ten commandments, all the material about building a tabernacle and its furnishings, and the golden calf episode.

Leviticus: 13:1–2, 44–46; 19:1–2, 11–18; 23:4–11, 26–27, 33–37; 25:1, 8–17.

Leviticus: 1:1—12:8; 13:3–43, 47—18:30; 19:3–10, 19—23:3, 12–14, 17–25, 28–32, 38—24:23; 25:2–7, 18—27:34.

Leviticus Conclusion: Except for information on leprosy, another version of the ten commandments, and holy days, there is very little of the HB (OT) book of Leviticus in the Lectionary. While the book consists of Jewish law as a way of life, none of that material is found in the Lectionary.

Numbers: 3:5–9; 6:22–27; 11:4b–17, 24–30; 12:1–13; 13:1–2, 25—14:1, 26–29, 34–35; 20:1–13; 21:4–9; 24:2–7, 15–17b.

Numbers: 1:1—3:4, 10—6:21; 7:1—11:4a, 18–23, 31–35; 12:14–16; 13:3–24; 14:2–25, 30–33, 36—19:22; 20:14—21:3, 10—24:1, 8–14, 17c—36:13.

Numbers Conclusion: As can be concluded by comparing **Numbers** to *Numbers* above, very little of this HB (OT) book can be found in the Lectionary.

Deuteronomy: 1:9–14; 4:1–2, 5–9, 32–40; 5:12–15; 6:1–13; 7:6–11; 8:2–3, 7–18; 10:8–9, 12–22; 11:18, 26–28, 32; 18:15–20; 24:17–22; 26:4–10, 16–19; 30:1–4, 10—31:8; 32:1–43; 34:1–12.

Deuteronomy: 1:1–8, 15—3:29; 4–4, 10–31, 41—5:11, 16–33; 6:14—7:5, 12—8:1, 4–6, 19—10:7, 10–11; 11:1–17, 19–25, 29–31; 12:1—18:14, 21—24:16; 25:1—26:3, 11–15; 27:1—29:28; 30:5–9; 31:9–30; 32:44—33:29.

Deuteronomy Conclusion: As the name of this HB (OT) book indicates, this second edition of the Law or Torah presents Moses speaking to the Israelites before he dies and they cross the Jordan River into the Promised Land under the leadership of Joshua. While there are several passages from the book incorporated into the Lectionary, the majority of the book remains unused.

Joshua: 3:7–11, 13–17; 5:9–12; 8:30–35; 24:1–29.

Joshua: 1:1—3:6; 4:1—5:8, 13—8:29; 9:1—23:16; 24:30–33.

Joshua Conclusion: As can be seen, in three years very little from the HB (OT) book of Joshua is contained in the Lectionary. In fact, except for a few representative passages, most of the book of Joshua does not make it into the Lectionary.

Judges: 2:11–19; 6:11–24a; 9:6–15; 11:29–39a; 13:2–7.

Judges: 1:1—2:10, 20—6:10, 24b—9:5, 16—11:28, 39b—13:1, 8–23; 14:1—21:25.

Judges Conclusion: Like the HB (OT) book of Joshua, the book of twelve Judges is represented in the Lectionary only by Gideon—a small part of the whole story—and by Samson—a small part of the whole story. Nothing from Judges is read in the Sunday Cycles; pericopes found in the Lectionary are read in the Weekday Years.

Ruth: 1:1–6, 14–16, 22—2:3, 8–11; 4:13–17.

Ruth: 1:2, 7–13, 17–21; 2:4–7, 12—4:12, 18–22.

Ruth Conclusion: Even though the HB (OT) book of Ruth is only four chapters long, only a small part of the whole story of Ruth, Naomi, and Boaz is given. The process of how Ruth marries Boaz and they become the parents of Obed, who becomes the father of Jesse, the father of King David is omitted. Nothing from Ruth is read in the Sunday Cycles; pericopes found in the Lectionary are read in the Weekday Years.

1 Samuel: 1:1–22, 24—2:10; 3:1–10, 19–20; 4:1–11; 8:4–7, 10—9:4, 17–19; 10:1a; 15:16–23; 16:1–13; 17:32–33, 37, 40–51; 18:6–9; 19:1–7; 24:3–21; 26:2, 7–9, 12–13, 22–23.

1 Samuel: 1:23, 2:11–36; 3:11–18, 21; 4:12—8:3, 8–9; 9:5–16, 20–27; 10:1b—15:15, 24–35; 16:14—17:31, 34–36, 38–39, 52—18:5, 10–30; 19:8—24:2, 22—26:1, 3–6, 10–11, 14–21, 24—31:13.

1 Samuel Conclusion: While there seems to be many pericopes read from the HB (OT) First Book of Samuel, only a small portion of the book is presented in the Lectionary. What is contained

in the Lectionary primarily concerns Samuel and his anointing of Saul and David as kings of all Israel.

2 Samuel: 1:1–4, 11–12, 19, 21–27; 5:1–7, 10; 6:12–15, 17–19; 7:1–19, 24, 29; 11:1–10, 13–17; 12:1–7a, 10–17; 15:13–14, 30; 16:5–13; 18:9–10, 14, 24–25, 30—19:3; 24:2, 9–17.

2 Samuel: 1:5–10, 13–18, 20–22; 2:1—4:12; 5:8–9, 11—6:12, 20–23; 7:20–23, 25–28; 8:1—10:19; 11:11–12, 18–27; 12:7b–9, 18—15:12, 15–29, 31—16:4, 13—18:8, 11–13, 15–23, 26–29; 19:4—24:1, 3–8, 18–25.

2 Samuel Conclusion: After reporting Saul's death, a representative sample of pericopes from the HB (OT) Second Book of Samuel are found in the Lectionary. They are focused on King David, his bringing of the Ark to Jerusalem, his sin with Bathsheba, and the internal strife among his family. Many of the passages in the Lectionary are pieced-together; they omit verses in order to present a new, streamlined story heard (read) only in the Weekday Years.

1 Kings: 2:1–4, 10–12; 3:4–14; 8:1–7, 9–13, 22–23, 27–30, 41–43, 55–61; 10:1–10; 11:4–13, 26–32; 12:19, 26–32; 13:33–34; 17:1–24; 18:20–39; 41—19:9, 11–16, 19–21; 21:1–29.

1 Kings: 1:1–53; 2:5–9, 13—3:3, 15—7:51, 8, 14–21, 24–26, 31–40, 44–54, 62—9:28; 10:11—11:3, 14–25, 33—12:18, 20–25, 33—13:32; 14:1—16:34; 18:1–19, 40; 19:10, 17–18; 20:1–42; 22:1–54.

1 Kings Conclusion: After presenting some of King David's last words and his appointment of Solomon as the son to succeed him, the Lectionary contains pericopes about King Solomon from the HB (OT) First Book of Kings. However, it omits his building of the Temple and focuses only on the dedication of the Temple and pieced-together verses of his prayer. It seems to present in passing the dissolution of his kingdom after his death. The embedded narrative about the prophets Elijah and Elisha have a better representation in the Lectionary, but not all of their stories are found in the Lectionary.

2 Kings: 2:1, 6–14; 4:8–11, 14–16a, 18–21, 32–37, 42—5:17; 11:1–4, 9–18, 20; 17:5–8, 13–15a, 18; 19:10–21, 31–36, 20:1–6; 22:8–13; 23:1–3; 24:8–17; 25:1–12.

2 Kings: 1:1–18; 2:2–5, 15—4:7, 12–13, 16b–17, 21b–31, 38–41; 5:18—10:36; 11:5–8, 19; 12:1—17:4, 9–12, 15b–17, 19—19:9a, 12–13, 22–30, 37; 20:7–22:7, 14–20; 23:4–24:7, 18–20; 25:13–30.

2 Kings Conclusion: The HB (OT) Second Book of Kings continues the narrative about the prophets Elijah and Elisha with several pericopes in the Lectionary. Other important historical incidents are presented beside the mention of the some of the kings of Israel and Judah; however, most of the material concerning the kings—after whom the book is named—is omitted in the Lectionary.

1 Chronicles: 15:3–4, 15–16; 16:1–2; 29:10–13.

1 Chronicles: 1:1—15:2, 5–14, 17–29; 16:3—29:9, 14–30.

1 Chronicles Conclusion: Because the HB (OT) First Book of Chronicles contains material similar to that found in First and Second Samuel and the First Book of Kings, only a few pericopes are found in the Lectionary for Weekday Years. Nothing is read from First Chronicles in Sunday Cycles.

2 Chronicles: 5:6–10, 13—6:2; 24:17–25; 36:14–16, 19–23.

2 Chronicles: 1:1—5:4, 11–12; 6:3—24:16, 26—36:13, 17–18.

2 Chronicles Conclusion: Because the HB (OT) Second Book of Chronicles contains material similar to that found in the Second Book of Kings, only a few pericopes are found in the Lectionary for Weekday Years. Only one passage is read from Second Chronicles during Sunday Cycle B.

Ezra: 1:1–6; 6:7–8, 12b, 14–20; 9:5–9.

Ezra: 1:7—6:6, 9–12a, 13, 21—9:4, 10—10:44.

Ezra Conclusion: Three short passages from the HB (OT) book of Ezra are found in the Weekday Years in the Lectionary. Most of Ezra is not read (heard).

Nehemiah: 2:1–9; 7:72b—8:4a, 5–6; 7b–12.

Nehemiah: 1:1–11; 2:9—7:72a; 8:4b, 7a, 13—13:31.

Nehemiah Conclusion: Three pericopes are extracted from the HB (OT) book of Nehemiah. One is read (heard) in the Sunday Cycle C, and two are read in Weekday Year I. Most of Nehemiah is not read (heard).

Tobit: 1:1–3; 2:1—3:11, 16–17a; 6:10–11; 7:1abc, 5b–17; 8:4–9; 11:5–17; 12:1, 5–15, 20; 13:1–9.

Tobit: 1:4–22; 3:11b–15, 17bc—6:9, 12–18; 7:1d–5a; 8:1–3, 10—11:4, 18; 12:2–4, 16–19, 21–22; 13:10—14:15.

Tobit Conclusion: The OT (A) book of Tobit is a novella; since the Lectionary presents only the basic pieces of the plot structure, it omits parts of the story in favor of presenting the outline of the book. In other words, the whole novella is not read.

Judith:

Judith: 1:1—16:25

Judith Conclusion: There is nothing in the Lectionary from the OT (A) book of Judith, which is a novella, like Tobit. Because Judith is longer than Tobit, a number of pericopes would have to be chosen to give a sampling of the contents of the book.

Esther: C:12, 14–16, 23–25.

Esther: A:1—C:11, 13, 17–22, 26—F:10.

Esther Conclusion: Only one pieced-together pericope from the HB (OT) book of Esther appears in the Lectionary. Because the Catholic Hebrew Bible (Christian Old Testament) edition of

Esther differs from the Hebrew (Jewish) Bible edition of Esther, the material from the Catholic Hebrew Bible that is added to the Jewish Hebrew Bible form of the book uses capital letters to indicate the additional material.

1 Maccabees: 1:10–15, 41–43, 54–57, 62–63; 2:15–29, 49–52, 57–64; 4:36–37, 52–59; 6:1–13.

1 Maccabees: 1:1–9, 16–40, 44–53, 58–61; 2:1–14, 30–48, 53–56, 65—4:35, 38–51, 60—5:68; 6:14–16:24.

1 Maccabees Conclusion: Only four pericopes are taken from the OT (A) book of First Maccabees, and those are found in Weekdays Year I. No passages from First Maccabees are found in the Sunday Cycles. More of the book needs to be read for no other reason than to understand the many historical characters presented in the chapters of the book and what each represents.

2 Maccabees: 2:18b–31; 6:18—7:2, 9–14, 20–31.

2 Maccabees: 1:1—2:17, 32—6:17; 7:3–8, 15–19, 32—16:39.

2 Maccabees Conclusion: While there are three passages chosen from the OT (A) book of Second Maccabees for the Lectionary, one of them is read in Sunday Cycle C, and two of them are read in Weekdays Year I. All three pericopes are heavily edited and form pieced-together passages from verses that create a new story out of an old one. Most of the riches of the Second Book of Maccabees is left undiscovered (unread, unheard).

Job: 1:6–22; 3:1–3, 11–17, 20–23; 7:1–4, 6–21; 9:1–12, 14–16; 19:1, 21–27; 31:16–20, 24–25, 31–32; 38:1, 8–21; 40:3–5; 42:1–6, 12–16.

Job: 1:1–5; 2:1–13; 3:4–10, 18–19, 24—6:30; 7:5; 8:1–22; 9:13, 17—18:21; 19:2–20, 26—31:15, 21–23, 26–30, 33—37:24; 38:2–7, 22—40:2, 6—41:26; 42:7–11, 17.

Job Conclusion: If there is any biblical book that the Lectionary violates the context of its verses, it is the HB (OT) book of Job.

Pericopes chosen from Job for the Lectionary are heavily edited; large segments of verses in speeches are omitted, changing the tone and the message of the speech. The organization of the book into cycles of speeches is ignored, one cannot tell who is saying what, and there is more focus on what the LORD—even God's speeches are edited—says than on what other characters, including Job, say in the book. The wisdom that the book of Job is designed to impart is reduced to eight passages in the Lectionary: two pericopes are read during Sunday Cycle B, and six are read during Weekdays Year II.

Psalms: 1, 2, 3, 4, 5, 6, 7, 8, 9, 10, 12, 13, 15, 16, 17, 18, 19, 21, 22, 23, 24, 25, 26, 27, 28, 29, 30, 31, 32, 33, 34, 36, 37, 40, 41, 42, 43, 44, 45, 46, 47, 48, 49, 50, 51, 52, 54, 55, 56, 57, 59, 60, 61, 62, 63, 65, 66, 67, 68, 69, 71, 72, 74, 77, 78, 79, 80, 81, 82, 84, 85, 86, 87, 88, 89, 90, 91, 92, 93, 94, 95, 96, 97, 98, 99, 100, 101, 102, 103, 104, 105, 106, 107, 109, 110, 111, 112, 113, 114, 115, 116, 117, 118 119, 121, 122, 123, 124, 126, 127, 128, 130, 131, 132, 135, 136, 137, 138, 139, 141, 143, 144, 145, 146, 147, 148, 149, 150.

Psalms: 11, 14, 20, 35, 38, 39, 53, 58, 64, 70, 73, 75, 76, 83, 108, 120, 125, 129, 133, 134, 140, 142.

Psalms Conclusion: Verses from Psalms are used with a Lectionary-provided refrain as a response to the First Reading. The six-to ten-verses chosen echo something from the reading. Unless the psalm is short, not all the verses of a psalm may be used, and some verses of some psalms are used multiple times throughout the three-year Sunday Cycle and the two-year Weekdays Years, while some verses are never used. Also, some verses of a psalm may be used one time, and other verses from the same psalm may be used another time. The list above presents the number of the whole psalm that is used or omitted over three years. Analysis of the verses of Psalms employed in the Lectionary and those omitted would result in a book.

Proverbs: 2:1–9; 3:27–34; 4:7–13; 8:22–23, 28–31; 9:1–6; 21:1–6, 10–13; 30:5–9; 31:10–13, 19–20, 30–31.

Proverbs: 1:1–33; 2:10—3:26; 4:1–6, 14—8:21, 24–27, 32–36; 9:7—20:30; 21:7–9, 14—30:4, 10—31:9, 14–18, 21–29.

Proverbs Conclusion: Only six pericopes represent the HB (OT) book of Proverbs in the Lectionary. One passage appears in Sunday Cycle A, one in Sunday Cycle B, and one in Sunday Cycle C. The other three passages appear in Weekdays Year II. The pericopes from Proverbs provides only a sampling of what the total book contains.

Ecclesiastes: 1:2–11; 2:1–23; 3:1–11; 11:9—12:8.

Ecclesiastes: 1:1, 12–18; 2:24–26; 3:12—11:8; 12:9–14.

Ecclesiastes Conclusion: Only four passages are found in the Lectionary from the HB (OT) book of Ecclesiastes. Three are read in Weekdays Year II and one in Sunday Cycle C. The four pericopes from this book provide only a sampling from the book and do not present the depth of wisdom literature displayed by a complete reading of the book.

Song of Songs: 2:8–14, 16; 3:1–4a; 8:6–7.

Song of Songs: 1:1—2:7; 2:15, 17; 3:4b—8:5, 8–14

Song of Songs Conclusion: The Lectionary contains one pieced-together pericope taken from the HB (OT) book of the Song of Songs, and that passage is read in both Weekdays Year I and II. No material from the Song of Songs is read (heard) in the Sunday Cycles. The context of the various love poems contained in the book is ignored by the Lectionary.

Wisdom: 1:1–7, 13–15; 2:1a, 12—3:9; 4:7–14; 6:1–16; 7:7–10, 15–16, 22—8:1; 9:9–11, 13–18; 11:22-—12:2, 13, 16–19; 13:1–9; 18:6–9, 14–16; 19:6–9.

Wisdom: 1:8–12, 16; 2:1b–11; 3:10—4:6, 16—5:23; 6:17—7:6, 11–14, 17–21; 8:2—9:8, 12; 10:1—11:21; 12:3–12, 14–15, 20–27; 13:10—18:5, 10–13, 17—19:5, 10–22.

Wisdom Conclusion: Sixteen passages are found in the Lectionary from the OT (A) book of Wisdom. Seven are read in Weekdays Year I; one, a duplicate of one read in Year I, is read in Year II, and two are read in Sunday Cycle A, three in Sunday Cycle B, and three in Sunday Cycle C. The sixteen pericopes from this book provide only a sampling from the book and do not present the depth of wisdom literature displayed by a complete reading of the book. The pericopes chosen from the book for the Lectionary are usually pieced-together verses, which create a passage that is not biblical.

Sirach (Ecclesiasticus): 1:1–10; 2:1–13; 3:3–7, 14–26, 30; 4:12–22; 5:1–10; 6:5–17; 15:1–6, 16–20; 17:1–13, 20–27; 24:1–7, 12–16, 26–30; 26:1–4, 16–20; 27:5–8; 28:1–9; 35:1–17, 20–22; 36:1–2, 5–6, 13–19; 39:1, 5–14; 42:15–25; 44:1, 9–15; 47:2–13; 48:1–15; 51:1–27.

Sirach (Ecclesiasticus): 1:11–29; 2:14—3:2, 8–13, 27–29; 4:1–11, 23–31; 5:11—6:4, 18—14:27; 15:7–15; 16:1–28; 17:14–19; 18:1—23:27; 24:8–11, 17–23, 31—25:25; 26:5–15; 27:1–4, 9–30; 28:10—34:26; 35:18–19, 23–24; 36:3–4, 7–12, 20—38:34; 39:2–4, 15—42:14; 43:1–35; 44:2–8, 16—47:1, 14–25; 48:16—50:23, 27–29; 51:28–30.

Sirach (Ecclesiasticus) Conclusion: While there are twenty-seven passages from the OT (A) book of Sirach (Ecclesiasticus) in the Lectionary, they represent only a few verses from the fifty-one chapters of this wisdom-literature book. Pericopes from Sirach are found in all Sunday Cycles and both Weekday Years. While the pericopes from this book provide a good sampling from the book, they do not present the depth of wisdom literature displayed by a complete reading of the book. And as noted in other wisdom literature books, some of the passages are pieced together from non-sequential verses to create a reading that does not exist in the book.

Isaiah: 1:10–20; 2:1–5; 4:2—5:7; 6:1–8; 7:1–14; 8:10, 23—9:6; 10:5–7, 13–16; 11:1–10, 13—12:6; 22:19–23; 25:6–10; 26:1–9, 12, 16–19; 29:17–24; 30:19–21, 23–26; 32:15–18; 35:1–10; 38:1–8, 10–21; 40:1–11, 25–31; 41:8–10, 13–20; 42:1–7; 43:16–22, 24b–25; 44:1–5; 45:1, 4–8, 18, 21b–25; 48:17–19; 49:1–6, 8–15; 50:4–9a; 52:7–10, 13—54:14; 55:1—56:3a, 6–8; 57:15–19; 58:1–14; 60:1–6; 61:1–3ab, 6a, 8b—62:5, 11–12; 63:7–9, 16–17, 19b; 64:2–7, 17–21; 66:10–14, 18–21.

Isaiah: 1:1–9, 21–31; 2:6—4:1; 5:8–30; 6:9–13; 7:15—8:9, 11–20; 9:7—10:4, 8–12, 17–34; 11:11–12; 13:1—22:18, 24—25:5, 10b–12; 26:10–11, 13–15, 20—29:16; 30:1–18, 22, 27—32:14, 19–20; 33:1—34:17; 36:1—37:38; 38:21; 39:1–8; 40:12–24; 41:1–5, 11–12, 21–29; 42:8—43:15, 23–24a, 26–28; 44:6–28; 45:2–3, 9–17, 19–21; 46:1—48:16, 20–22; 49:7, 16—50:3, 9b—52:6, 11–12; 54:15–17; 56:3b–5, 9—57:14, 20–21; 59:1–21; 60:7–22; 61:3c–5, 6b–8; 62:6–10; 63:1–6, 10–15, 18–19a; 64:1, 8—65:16, 22—66:9, 15–17, 22–24.

Isaiah Conclusion: While there are 118 passages from the HB (OT) book of the prophet Isaiah—the most pericopes from any HB (OT) book in the Lectionary—twenty-five of them are duplicates read in the Sunday Cycles A, B, and C or in the Weekday Year I and II. Other than the duplicates, other pericopes from the prophet Isaiah appear in all three Sunday Cycles and both Weekday Years. However, material in the Lectionary from Isaiah, represents only a sampling of this sixty-six-chapter book. There is a focus on the messianic material early in the book and the glory of the restored Jerusalem at the end of the book. Material dealing with punishment or destruction is omitted from the Lectionary.

Jeremiah: 1:1, 4—2:3, 7–8, 12–13; 3:14–17; 7:1–11, 23–28; 11:18; 13:1–11; 14:17–22; 15:10, 16–21; 17:5–10; 18:1–6, 18–20; 20:7–13;

23:1–8; 26:1–9, 11–16, 24; 28:1–17; 30:1–2, 12–15, 18–22; 31:1–14, 31–37; 33:14–16; 38:4–6, 8–10.

Jeremiah: 1:2–3; 2:4–6, 9–11, 14—3:13, 18—6:30; 7:12–22, 29—11:17; 12:1–17; 13:12—14:16; 15:1–9, 11, 15; 16:1—17:4, 11–27; 18:7–17, 21—20:6, 14—22:30; 23:9—25:38; 26:10, 17–23; 27:1–22; 29:1–32; 30:3–11, 16–17, 23–24; 31:15–30, 38—33:13, 17—38:3, 7, 11—52:34.

Jeremiah Conclusion: Of the thirty-four passages from the HB (OT) book of Jeremiah, twenty of them are read (heard) in Weekday Year II. Five are duplicates also read (heard) in Weekday I. Two are read (heard) in Sunday Cycle A, three in Sunday Cycle B, and four in Sunday Cycle C. Many of the passages consist of pieced-together verses that create a Lectionary pericope that is not a biblical pericope. Much of the fifty-two chapters of the prophet Jeremiah is not found in the Lectionary.

Lamentations: 2:2, 10–14, 18–19; 3:17–26.

Lamentations: 1:1—2:1, 3–9, 15–17, 20—3:16, 27—5:22

Lamentations Conclusion: Only one pieced-together pericope from the HB (OT) book of Lamentations is found in the Lectionary during Weekday Year II. A single passage does not represent the contents of the short book.

Baruch: 1:15–22; 3:9–15, 32—4:12, 27–29; 5:1–9.

Baruch: 1:1–14; 2:1—3:8, 16–31; 4:13–26, 30–37; 6:1–72.

Baruch Conclusion: The OT (A) book of the prophet Baruch is represented with four passages in the Lectionary. Two are read (heard) during Weekday Year I, one is read (heard) during Sunday Cycle C, and the same pericope is read (heard) during Sunday Cycle A, B, and C. The pericopes are pieced-together verses that create a new reading that is not found in the Bible.

Ezekiel: 1:2–5, 24–28a; 2:2–5, 8—3:4, 17–21; 9:1–7; 10:18–22; 12:1–12; 16:1–15, 59–63; 17:22–24; 18:1–10, 13b, 21–28, 30–32; 24:15–24; 28:1–10; 33:7–9; 34:1–17; 36:16–17a, 18–28; 37:1–19, 21–28; 43:1–7a; 47:1–9, 12.

Ezekiel: 1:1, 6–23, 28b—2:1, 6–7; 3:5–15, 22—8:18; 9:8—10:17, 23—11:21; 12:13—15:8; 16:16—58; 17:1–21; 18:11–20; 19:1—24:14, 25—27:36; 28:11—33:6, 10–33; 34:18—36:15, 17b, 29–38; 37:20; 38:1—42:20; 43:7b—46:24; 47:10–11, 13—48:35.

Ezekiel Conclusion: The HB (OT) prophet Ezekiel fares the best for pericopes spread throughout the Lectionary. Sixteen passages are read (heard) in Weekday Year II and three in Weekday Year I. Six passages are read (heard) in Sunday Cycle A, four in Sunday Cycle B, and three in Sunday Cycle C. Two passages are duplicates read (heard) in all three Sunday Cycles. The total number of passages—thirty-two—however, give only a sample of the forty-eight chapters of the book.

Daniel: 1:1–6, 8–21; 2:31–45; 3:14–20, 25, 34–43, 52–88, 91–92, 95; 5:1–6, 13–14, 16–17, 23–28; 6:12–28; 7:2–27; 9:4–10; 12:1–3; 13:1–9, 15–17, 19–30, 33–62.

Daniel: 1:7; 2:1–30, 46–49; 3:1–13, 21–24, 26–33, 44–51, 89–90, 93–94, 96—4:34, 5:7–12, 15, 18–22, 29—6:11, 29—7:1, 28—9:3, 11—11:45; 12:4–13; 13:10–14, 17–18, 31–32, 63—14:42.

Daniel Conclusion: While the twenty-two passages chosen from the HB (OT) book of the prophet Daniel represent a good sampling of the material in this book, the pericopes read (heard), except for two in Sunday Cycle B, are in Weekday I and II, and three of them are duplicates. In order to shorten some of the stories, the introductory material has been removed. For example, the first thirty verses of chapter 2 about the king's dream does not appear in the Lectionary; only verses 31 through 45, the interpretation of the king's dream by Daniel, form the reading. Likewise, the result of Daniel's interpretation of the king's dream (2:46–49) is omitted from the Lectionary. While much of the prophet is presented in the Lectionary, the context for each of the accounts is omitted.

Hosea: 2:16, 17b–18, 21–22; 6:1–6; 8:4–7, 11–13, 10:1–3, 7–8, 12; 11:1–4; 8c–9; 14:2–10.

Hosea: 1:1—2:15, 17a, 19–20, 23—5:15; 6:7—8:3, 8–10, 14—9:17; 10:4–6, 9–11, 13–15; 11:5–8ab, 10—14:1.

Hosea Conclusion: Eleven pieced-together pericopes are scattered through the Lectionary. One occurs in Sunday Cycle A, two in Sunday Cycle B, six in Weekday Year II, and two duplicate passages in Weekday Year I. Except for four and one-half verses all of chapters 1 and 2 are omitted; since introductory material in a biblical book gives direction to the work, the new passage created from the four and one-half verses from chapter 2 removes all trace of the contents that follow in the twelve remaining chapters of the work.

Joel: 1:13–15; 2:1–2, 12–18, 21–24, 26—3:5; 4:12–21.

Joel: 1:1–12, 16–20; 2:3–11, 19–20, 25; 4:1–11.

Joel Conclusion: In the Sunday Cycle A, B, and C, one pieced-together passage is read (heard) in all three cycles. In Weekday Year I, three passages are read (heard) and one is duplicated in Weekday Year II. Like Hosea above, the introductory material that gives the context for the prophet's work, chapter 1, is omitted except for three continuous verses, which serve as a call to penance addressed to the priests. Likewise, the material that introduces the judgment of the nations in chapter 4 omits verses 1 through 11, which set the context for verses 12 through 21.

Amos: 2:6–10, 13—3:9; 4:11–12; 5:4, 14–15, 21–24; 6:1a, 4–7; 7:10–16; 8:4–6, 9–12; 9:11–15.

Amos: 1:1—2:5, 11–12; 3:9—4:10, 13—5:3, 5–13, 16–20, 2527: 6:1b–3, 8—7:9; 8:1–3, 7–8, 13–14; 9:1–10.

Amos Conclusion: The HB (OT) book of the prophet Amos is another work whose introductory material is not contained in the Lectionary. Most of what has been chosen from Amos are short passages in Weekday Year II designed to give a sample of the book. The one passage that appears in Sunday Cycle B and the two that appear in Sunday Cycle C are designed to echo something in the gospel pericope assigned to the given days.

Obadiah:

Obadiah: 1:1–21

Obadiah Conclusion: The sternness of the HB (OT) book of the prophet Obadiah is totally ignored by the Lectionary. Nothing from the book is found in the Lectionary.

Jonah: 1:1—2:8, 11—4:11.

Jonah: 2:9–10

Jonah Conclusion: Only two verses of the four-chapter HB (OT) book of the prophet Jonah is not read (heard) from the Lectionary! One passage is read (heard) in Sunday Cycle B, four passages are read (heard) in Weekday Year I and a duplicate from Year I in Year II. Jonah is the most complete biblical book read (heard) in the Lectionary.

Micah: 2:1–5; 4:1–4; 5:1–4a; 6:1–4, 6–8; 7:7–9, 14–15, 18–20

Micah: 1:1–16; 2:6—3:12, 5–14; 5:4bc–14; 6:5, 9—7:6, 10–13, 16–17.

Micah Conclusion: Only samples from the HB (OT) prophet Micah are contained in the Lectionary. The introductory material, which sets the context for the book, is not included. Pieced-together passages give a message and tone that is not found when reding (hearing) the edited verses.

Nahum: 2:1–3; 3:1–3, 6–7.

Nahum: 1:1–14; 2:4–14; 3:4–5, 8–19.

Nahum Conclusion: Only one pieced-together passage from the HB (OT) three-chapter-prophet Nahum is found in the Lectionary. All of chapter 1, which gives the context for the book, is omitted along with all else, except for the passage created from eight verses in chapters 2 and 3.

Habakkuk: 1:2–3, 12—2:4

Habakkuk: 1:1, 4–11; 2:5—3:19.

Habakkuk Conclusion: The HB (OT) prophet Habakkuk's three-chapter book fares much better than his predecessor Nahum. From Habakkuk two pericopes are found in the Lectionary. One passage is read (heard) in Sunday Cycle C and one in Weekday Year II.

Zephaniah: 2:3–13; 3:1–2, 9–20.

Zephaniah: 1:1—2:2, 14–15; 3:3–8.

Zephaniah Conclusion: The short, three-chapter HB (OT) book of the prophet Zephaniah has passages taken from it and placed in the Lectionary. One pericope appears in Sunday Year A, and one appears in Sunday Year C. Also, the same two passages that appear in Weekday Year I also appear in Weekday Year II. However, all of the opening chapter, which sets the theme, tone, and context for the book is omitted.

Haggai: 1:1–8, 15—2:9.

Haggai: 1:9–14; 2:10–23.

Haggai Conclusion: While the beginning of the HB (OT) prophetic book of Haggai is found in the Lectionary, only two pericopes are read (heard) during Weekday Year I. The end of the book of the prophet Haggai (2:10–23) is not found in the Lectionary.

Zechariah: 2:5–9, 14–17; 8:1–8, 20–23; 9:9–10; 12:10–11; 13:1, 6–7.

Zechariah: 1:1—2:4, 10–13; 3:1—7:14; 8:9–19; 9:1–8, 11—12:9, 12–13; 13:2–5, 8—14:21.

Zechariah Conclusion: While the HB (OT) book of the prophet Zechariah is much longer than the six prophets preceding it, only one passage appears in Sunday Cycle A and one passage in Sunday Cycle C. Three pericopes are found in Weekday Year I. Not only is all the opening chapter and the first four verses of chapter 2 omitted, but the pericopes that are chosen focus on the messianic restoration of Jerusalem. Much of the book, which is devoted to other topics, is omitted.

Malachi: 1:14b—2:2a, 8–10; 3:1–4, 13–20a, 23–24.

Malachi: 1:1–14a; 2:2b–7, 11–17; 3:5–12, 20b–22.

Malachi Conclusion: The context found in the opening chapter of the HB (OT) book of the prophet Malachi is omitted in the Lectionary. Five pericopes are found in the Lectionary: one each in Sunday Cycle A and C, two in Weekday Year I, and a repeat of one found in Weekday Year I in Year II.

Matthew: 1:1—4:17, 23—12:8, 14–21, 38–42, 46—15:2, 10–14, 21–37; 16:13—18:5, 10—20:28; 21:1–11, 23–43, 45—22:21, 34–40; 23:1–32; 24:4–14, 37—25:46; 26:14—28:20.

Matthew: 4:18–22; 12:9–13, 22–37, 43–45; 15:3–9, 15–20, 38—16:12; 18:6–9; 20:29–34; 21:12–22; 22:23–33, 41–45; 23:33—24:3, 15–36; 26:1–13.

Matthew Conclusion: Not all of the CB (NT) Gospel according to Matthew is read (heard) during the Sunday Cycle A, when it is heard (read) almost exclusively nor during Ordinary Time weeks 10 through 21 in Weekday Year I and II. Much of the writer's single-verse commentary is omitted, along with other material that could be offensive to readers (hearers).

Mark: 1:1—12:44; 13:24—16:20.

Mark: 13:1–23; 16:20b.

Mark Conclusion: The only material not read in the CB (NT) Gospel according to Mark consists of verses 1 through 23 of chapter 13, known by biblical scholars as the Little Apocalypse and verse 16:20b, known as the shorter ending, one of three endings for Mark's Gospel. The Little Apocalypse gives information useful in dating Mark's Gospel. Mark's Gospel is read (heard) almost exclusively in Sunday Cycle B and in Ordinary Time weeks 1 through 9 in Weekday Years I and II.

Luke: 1:1–79; 2:1–14, 15b—3:18, 21—7:17, 18b—8:21; 9:1–9, 11b–26, 28–36, 43b—11:32, 37—12:21, 32—14:33; 15:1—16:15, 19—18:14, 35—19:48; 20:27-40; 21:1–36; 22:14—24:53.

Luke: 1:80; 2:15a; 3:19 20; 7:18a; 8:22–56; 9:10–11a, 27, 37–43a; 11:33–36; 12:22–31; 14:34–35; 16:16–18; 18:15–34; 20:1–26, 41–47; 21:37—22:13.

Luke Conclusion: As can be easily determined by comparing **Luke** to *Luke* above, not all of the CB (NT) Gospel according to Luke is read (heard) during Sunday Year C, when it is used primarily, nor in Ordinary Time weeks 22 through 34 Weekday Years I and II. Material left out of the Lectionary consists of the author's narratives or material the author took from Mark's Gospel, one of his sources, and rewrote to fit his style. Before Luke's narrative about the baptism of Jesus (3:21-22), the Lectionary omits 3:19-20, very important information for the context in this gospel.

John: 1:1—2:11; 3:13–36; 4:5—6:69; 7:1–2, 10–18, 25–30, 34—8:42, 51—10:18, 22—12:16, 20–36a, 44—15:21, 26—16:4a, 5—20:29; 21:1–25.

John: 2:12; 4:1–4; 6:70–71; 7:3–9, 11–13, 19–24, 31–33; 8:43–50; 10:19–21; 12:17–19, 36b–43; 15:22–25; 16:4b; 20:30–31.

John Conclusion: The CB (NT) Gospel according to John is read (heard) at various times throughout the Sunday Cycles A, B, and

C, and during the Easter Season in both Weekday Years I and II. As can be concluded from comparing **John** and *John* above, verses that are not found in the Lectionary have to do with the narrator's comments and negative material spoken by the Johannine Jesus.

Acts: 1:1–17, 20—2:11, 14–22—4:21, 23–37; 5:12–26, 28—6:15; 7:44—8:8, 14–17, 26-—9:22, 26—10:1, 25–26, 33–48; 11:1—12:11, 24—13:5a, 13–39, 43–52; 14:5—15:31; 16:1–15, 22–34; 17:15, 22—18:18, 23—19:8; 20:17–38; 22:3–16, 30; 23:6–11; 25:13–21; 26:19–23; 28:7–20, 30–31.

Acts: 1:18–19; 2:12–13, 15–21; 4:22; 5:1–11, 27; 7:1–43; 8:9–13, 18–25; 9:23–25, 43; 10:2–24, 27–32; 12:12–23; 13:5b–12, 40–42; 14:1–4; 15:32–41; 16:16–21, 35—17:14, 16–21; 18:19–22; 19:9—20:16; 21:1—22:2, 17–29; 23:1–5, 12—25:12, 22—26:18, 24—28:6, 21–28.

Acts Conclusion: From chapter 19 to the end of the Acts of the Apostles at chapter 28, fewer pericopes are included in the Lectionary than from chapter 1 to chapter 18. It looks like the Lectionary ran out of room for passages from the CB (NT) Acts. Any material that might shed darkness on the apostles is not included in the Lectionary. Most of the lengthy discourse given by Stephen—a great summary of salvation history—is left out of the Lectionary. Likewise, while there is much attention given to Saul (Paul), much of the travelogue remains unused.

Romans: 1:1–7, 16–25; 2:1–11; 3:21–30; 4:1–8, 13, 16—5:16a, 17–21; 6:2–23; 7:18–25a; 8:1—9:5; 10:8–18; 11:1–2a, 11–12, 25—12:18; 13:8–13; 14:7–12; 15:4–9, 14–21; 16:3–9; 16a, 22–27.

Romans: 1:8–15, 26–32; 2:12—3:20, 31; 4:9–12, 14–15; 5:16b; 6:1; 7:1–17; 9:6—10:7, 19–21; 11:2b–10, 13–24; 12:19—13:7; 14:1–6, 13—15:3, 10–13, 22—16:2, 10–15, 17–21.

Romans Conclusion: The Lectionary omits the important section of the CB (NT) letter of Paul to the Romans which deals with freedom from Torah. By not including other sections of the letter, the Lectionary creates a letter within a letter and makes Paul write what he didn't write. Also omitted from the Lectionary is Paul's analogy of the olive tree and how both Jews and Gentiles will be saved. If one considers that Paul's letter to the Romans is one of the best exposes of his theology, then the editing done by the Lectionary changes the apostle's position in many ways. Paul's tight argument is loosened when parts of the letter are omitted. This means that Lectionary editors recreated Paul's letter to the Romans for the Lectionary to correspond to a theology that was not the author's. In other words, this letter is chopped into small pieces by the Lectionary, and some of the pieces are never read. Fifty-nine pericopes mean nothing out of their total-letter context.

1 Corinthians: 1:1–13, 17—3:11, 16—4:5, 6b–15; 5:1–8; 6:1–11, 13b–15a, 17 20; 7:25–35; 8:2–7, 11–13; 9:16–19, 22b–10:6, 10–12, 14–22, 31—11:1, 17–26, 33–34; 12:3b—13:13; 15:1–28, 35–37, 42–49, 51–58.

1 Corinthians: 1:14–16; 3:12–15; 4:6a, 16–21; 5:9–13; 6:12–13a, 15b–16; 7:1–24, 36—8:1, 8–10; 9:1–15, 20–22; 10:7–9, 13, 23–30; 11:2–16, 27–32; 12:1–3a; 14:1–40; 15:29–34, 38–41, 50; 16:1–24.

1 Corinthians Conclusion: As was noted above in the Romans Conclusion, the CB (NT) First Letter of Paul to the Corinthians creates readings out of non-consecutive verses. Furthermore, anything negative in the letter is removed from Lectionary passages. Paul's advice to the married is not included in the Lectionary, but his advice to virgins and widows is! Omitted are Paul's words about speaking in tongues (all of chapter 14) and the collection, travel plans, and conclusion (all of chapter 16). Thus, the fifty-four pericopes from Paul's First Letter to the Corinthians are not only spread over all three Sunday Cycles and Weekday Year II, but they are almost always out of context.

2 Corinthians: 1:1–7, 18–22; 3:1–11, 15—5:1, 6–10, 14—6:10; 8:1–15; 9:6–15; 10:17—11:11, 18, 21b–30; 12:1–10; 13:11–13.

2 *Corinthians*: 1:8–17, 23—2:17; 3:12–14; 5:2–5, 11–13; 6:11—7:16; 8:16—9:5; 10:1–16; 11:12–21a, 31–33; 12:11—13:10.

2 Corinthians Conclusion: Paul's Second Letter to the Corinthians in the CB (NT) contributes twenty-four pericopes to the Lectionary, spread over Sunday Cycles A, B, and C and Weekday Year I with one duplicate that appears in Year II. The Lectionary creates readings out of non-consecutive verses. As in the pericopes from First Corinthians, anything negative in Second Corinthians is not included in Lectionary passages. Paul's past relationship with the Corinthians is not included nor is his teaching about issues that cause friction between him and the Corinthians. Thus, large sections of the letter are not included in Lectionary pericopes. Pieced-together passages are always out of context and create a letter within a letter.

Galatians: 1:1–2, 6—2:2, 7–14, 16, 19—3:5, 7–14, 22–29; 4:4–8, 12–19, 22–24, 26–27, 31—5:6, 13–26; 6:14–18.

Galatians: 1:3–5; 2:3–6, 15, 17–18; 3:6, 15–21; 4:1–3, 9–11, 20–21, 25, 28–30; 5:7–12; 6:1–13.

Galatians Conclusion: Nineteen passages—many of them pieced-together verses—from Paul's letter to the Galatians are found in the Lectionary scattered through Sunday Cycles A, B, and C and Weekday Year II. As in other letters, negative material has not been included in the Lectionary. Also, as already noted, a letter within a letter has been created by the Lectionary. Furthermore, since Galatians is considered the second-best summary (Romans is first) of Pauline thought, the removal of Paul's words that Christ Jesus has surpassed the Law (Torah) should be included. While Paul is not antinomian, he did consider the time for the Law (Torah) to have passed.

Ephesians: 1:1–11, 13—2:22; 3:2—4:17, 20–24, 30—6:20.

Ephesians: 1:12; 3:1; 4:18–19, 25–29; 6:21–24.

Ephesians Conclusion: The letter to the Ephesians is a second-generation Pauline letter written by an unknown author who knew Paul's thought and who updated it for the late first or early second century, when a church structure was beginning to take place. With that background, it is hard to understand why so much of Ephesians has been contained in the Lectionary and so little of genuine Pauline letters (Romans, 1 and 2 Corinthians, Galatians, Philippians, First Thessalonians, and Philemon) has been contained in the Lectionary. Only thirteen verses of Ephesians are not contained in the Lectionary, which presents thirty-three pericopes from Ephesians spread all through Sunday Cycles A, B, and C, and Weekday Year II. Three pericopes are duplicates, appearing in all three Sunday Cycles.

Philippians: 1:1–11, 18c—2:18, 25–30; 3:3–14, 17—4:1, 4–21.

Philippians: 1:12–18ab; 2:19–24; 3:1–2, 15–16; 4:2–3, 22–23

Philippians Conclusion: All but nineteen verses of Paul's letter to the Philippians are contained in one of the nineteen passages in the Lectionary. As in other genuine Pauline letters, anything negative in the letter is not found in the Lectionary. Likewise, travel plans are not included in the Lectionary. Pericopes appear in Sunday Cycles A, B, and C, and In Weekday Year II.

Colossians: 1:1—2:3, 6–15; 3:1–21, 23–24.

Colossians: 2:4–5, 16–23: 3:22, 25—4:18.

Colossians Conclusion: Like Ephesians, the letter to the Colossians is a second-generation Pauline letter. Various short sections of the letter are omitted from the Lectionary, especially the advice given to slaves and slave masters! Also not included are the words about prayer and messages from and to several people at the end of the letter. Seven passages from Colossians are found in Sunday Cycle C, two of which are also found in Cycles A and B. Eight passages appear in Weekday Year I. As has been noted before, omitting verses not only creates a Scripture passage that does not exist, but it also creates a new letter within a letter.

1 Thessalonians: 1:1–5, 8—2:13; 3:7—5:6, 9–11, 16–24.

1 Thessalonians: 1:6–7; 2:14—3:6; 5:7–8, 12–15, 25–28.

1 Thessalonians Conclusion: Like other letters, anything negative in the CB (NT) First letter of Paul to the Thessalonians is omitted from pericopes in the Lectionary. Also, omitted are Paul's travel plans, exhortations about support, and the final greeting. Thus, a letter within a letter is created by the Lectionary.

2 Thessalonians: 1:1–5; 11—2:3a, 14—3:12, 16–18.

2 Thessalonians: 1:6–10; 2:3b–13; 3:13–15.

2 Thessalonians Conclusion: In the three-chapter, CB (NT), second-generation Pauline Second Letter to the Thessalonians, the Lectionary has omitted the material concerning God's wrath and punishment and how to treat those who do not follow the letter's contents. This results in a newly-created, positive teaching tool with all the negativity of the original removed.

1 Timothy: 1:1–2, 12–17; 2:1–8; 3:1–16; 4:12–16; 5:3–10; 6:2c–19.

1 Timothy: 1:3–11, 18–20; 2:9–15; 4:1–11; 5:1–2, 11—6:2ab, 20–21.

1 Timothy Conclusion: Eleven pericopes from the CB (NT) First Letter to Timothy are found in the Lectionary; three occur in Sunday Cycle C, and eight are found in Weekday Year I. The Lectionary does not include passages about teaching doctrine or the purpose of the law, the writer having condemned certain people, the way women should appear, the codes concerning young widows, presbyters, and slaves, but it does present qualifications for bishops and deacons! Because some of the qualifications for bishops—such as "married only once" (3:2)—no longer apply, it is interesting that this passage was not omitted from the Lectionary. In other words, very selective editing has taken place with concern that fluctuates

between ancient and modern culture. For example, why would the Lectionary contain pericopes about the qualifications for bishops and deacons but omit the same for presbyters? Or why would it contain pericopes about old widows but omit the same for young widows? Why are the rules for slaves omitted?

2 Timothy: 1:1–14; 2:1–3, 8–15; 3:8—4:8, 10–18.

2 Timothy: 1:15–18; 2:4–7, 16—3:7; 4:9, 19–22.

2 Timothy Conclusion: Nine pericopes from the CB (NT) Second Letter to Timothy are found in the Lectionary; one occurs in Sunday Cycle A, four occur in Sunday Cycle C, and four are found in Weekday Year II. As is found in other Lectionary passages taken from letters, the greeting or introduction is included, but the final greeting or conclusion is omitted. Words about the author's suffering, advice about soldiers and farmers, gossip, and moral depravity are omitted in Lectionary passages.

Titus: 1:1–9; 2:1–8, 11–14; 3:1–7.

Titus: 1:10–16; 2:9–10, 15; 3:8–15.

Titus Conclusion: Ten pericopes from the CB (NT) Letter to Titus are found in the Lectionary; two occur as duplicates in Sunday Cycles A, B, and C with one additional passage read (heard) in Year C, and three are found in Weekday Year II. Material omitted concerns the author's perspective on Jewish Christians, slaves, advice given to Titus, and the concluding greetings and blessings. While much of this three-chapter letter is including in the Lectionary, much has also been excluded.

Philemon: 1:7–20.

Philemon: 1:1–6, 21–25.

Philemon Conclusion: Because Paul's letter to Philemon, the only correspondence of the apostle to a single individual in the CB (NT), consists of one chapter, it provides only two passages in the

Lectionary: one in Sunday Cycle C and one in Weekday Year II. When compared to other genuine Pauline letters which retain the address and greetings in Lectionary pericopes, those are omitted in the two passages contained in the Lectionary. Also omitted are Paul's words of confidence, his intent to visit, and the final greetings. As noted several times above, these omitted verses create a letter within a letter that does not exist in the CB (NT).

Hebrews: 1:1–6; 2:5–12; 14–18; 3:7–14; 4:1–5, 11—5:10; 6:10—7:3, 15–17, 25—8:13; 9:2–3, 11–15, 24—10:25, 32—11:19, 32—12:15, 18–19, 21–24; 13:1–18, 20–21.

Hebrews: 1:7—2:4, 13; 3:1–6, 15–19; 4:6–10; 5:11—6:9; 7:4–14, 18–24; 9:1, 4–10, 16–23; 10:26–31; 11:20–31; 12:16–17, 20, 25–29; 13:19, 22–25.

Hebrews Conclusion: Even though the CB (NT) letter to the Hebrews is not a letter—it is a sermon, homily, or treatise—many of its HB (OT) quotations have been omitted from passages in the Lectionary. In other words, the prooftexting that the author employs to make his points has been removed from pericopes in the Lectionary. Hebrews contributes forty-seven pericopes to the Lectionary; two of them appear in all three Sunday Cycles. Only the two that appear in all three cycles are found in Sunday Cycle A; twelve passages are in Sunday Cycle B, and eight are in Cycle C. Twenty-five pericopes are found in Weekday Year I. Now matter how Hebrews is classified—sermon, homily, treatise, letter—a book within a book has been created by the Lectionary. There is a semi-continuous reading of the work, but much is omitted, and that affects the context of the passages that are included.

James: 1:1—2:9, 14–24, 26—3:10, 13—4:10, 13—5:20.

James: 2:10–13, 25; 3:11–12; 4:11–12

James Conclusion: All the CB (NT) letter of James—except for nine verses—appears in Lectionary pericopes. Interestingly, the pericope about the law, the mention of Rahab the harlot, the images of spring and the fig tree, and the exhortation not to speak evil of another are the nine verses that are omitted from the letter in the Lectionary. Nevertheless, the letter of James is the second most complete book taken from the Bible and used by the Lectionary; the first complete book is 1 John. Twelve passages appear in Weekday Year II, one in Sunday Cycle A, and five in Sunday Cycle B.

1 Peter: 1:3–25; 2:2–12, 20—3:9, 14–22; 4:7—5:4, 5b–14.

1 Peter: 1:1–2; 2:1, 13–19; 3:10–13; 4:1–6; 5:5a

1 Peter Conclusion: Unlike the letters in the Pauline corpus, the Catholic letters—James and 1 and 2 Peter—omit the opening greeting but include the concluding greeting! The CB (NT) First Letter of Peter contributes twelve pericopes to the Lectionary; six occur in Sunday Cycle A, one in Sunday Cycle B, and five in Weekday Year II. The material on citizenship and slavery is omitted; the negative evaluation of the Gentiles and the advice that younger members be subject to the presbyters is also omitted.

2 Peter: 1:2–7, 16–19; 3:8–15, 17–18.

2 Peter: 1:1, 8–15, 20—3:7, 16.

2 Peter Conclusion: As noted above, the opening greeting is omitted, but the concluding greeting is kept in the Lectionary pericopes extracted from the CB (NT) Second Letter of Peter. Anything negative in Second Peter is not found in Lectionary passages; this means that all of chapter 2 is omitted! Only three passages from Second Peter are found in the Lectionary: one in Sunday Cycle B, and two in Weekday Year II.

1 John: 1:1—5:21.

1 John:

1 John Conclusion: Every verse of the CB (NT) First Letter of John appears in thirty-seven pericopes in the Lectionary. There are two

in Sunday Cycle A, six in Sunday Cycle B, and one in Sunday Cycle C. The fourteen pericopes that appear in Weekday Year I are duplicated in Weekday Year II.

2 John: 1:4–9.

2 John: 1:1–3, 10–13.

2 John Conclusion: Only one passage from the CB (NT) Second Letter of John is found in the Lectionary in Weekday Year II. The first three verses of this one-chapter book are omitted as are the last four verses. In other words, all context has been removed from the pericope in the Lectionary.

3 John: 1:5–8.

3 John: 1:1–4, 9–15.

3 John Conclusion: Like the Second Letter of John above, the CB (NT) Third Letter of John gives one passage to the Lectionary in Weekday Year II. The first four verses of this one-chapter book are omitted, as are the last seven verses. Like Second John, all context has been removed from the pericope in the Lectionary.

Jude: 1:17, 21–25.

Jude: 1:1–16, 18–20.

Jude Conclusion: Like its biblical neighbors—Second John and Third John—the CB (NT) Letter of Jude is a one-chapter work which contributes one pericope to Weekday Year II. The six-verse edited pericope in the Lectionary has no context, since the opening material—the first sixteen verses—is not included in the passage.

Revelation: 1:1–13, 17–19; 2:1–4, 8–11; 3:1–6, 14—5:12; 7:2–4, 9–17; 8:3–4; 10:8–11; 11:4–12; 11:19b—12:12a; 14:1–3, 4b–5, 13–19; 15:1–4; 18:1–2, 21–23; 19:1–3, 5–9a; 20:1–4, 11—21:7, 9–14, 22–23; 22:1–7, 12–14, 16–17, 20–21.

Revelation: 1:14–16, 20; 2:5–7, 12–29; 3:7–13; 5:13—7:1, 5–8; 8:1–2, 5—10:7; 11:1–3, 13–19a; 12:12b—13:18; 14:4, 6–12, 20; 15:5—17:18; 18:3–20, 24; 19:4, 9b–21; 20:5–10; 21:8, 15–21, 24–27; 22:8–11, 15, 18–19.

Revelation Conclusion: In the Lectionary, the CB (NT) book of Revelation is very much carved into twenty-one pericopes scattered through Sunday Cycle B (1) and C (6), and Weekday Year II (13), with one passage repeated in Weekday Year I. In the first section of the book, seven churches are addressed, but the Lectionary omits Pergamum, Thyatira, and Philadelphia and any words about repentance. The material about the seals, the trumpets, the small scroll, the two witnesses, the beasts, the bowls, Babylon, the war, and more is omitted. The passages in the Lectionary create a new book of Revelation which does not exist. Those who selected passages from Revelation for the Lectionary would have done well to heed the authors words: "I warn everyone who hears the prophetic words in this book: if anyone adds to them, God will add to him the plagues described in this book, and if anyone takes away from the words in this prophetic book, God will take away his share in the tree of life and in the holy city described in this book" (22:18–19).

The *Lectionary* and the *Bible*

4

Advent Alternatives

(1) with Isaiah 1:1—21:17

(2) with Isaiah 22:1—41:12

(3) with Isaiah 41:21—66:24

(4) with Galatians, Ephesians, Philippians, Colossians,
1 Thessalonians, 2 Thessalonians, Titus, Philemon

Because the current First Reading pericopes for Advent (about four weeks before Christmas) are the same every year, what follows are alternative First Readings based on the principle of continuous or semi-continuous readings. In this Advent scenario, the gospel passages found in the Lectionary are not altered; only the

First Reading is altered. The following Advent alternatives can be considered alternate sets of First Readings for Advent that can be used by individuals, assigned by the administration of a church, or left to the choice of a pastor of a parish. The Second Reading on Sundays of Advent remains as in the Lectionary.

Advent Alternative 1

First Sunday of Advent: Isa 1:1–9 (indictment 1)

Monday of the First Week of Advent: Isa 1:21–31 (indictment 2)

Tuesday of the First Week of Advent: Isa 2:6–22 (idols)

Wednesday of the First Week of Advent: Isa 3:1–12 (crumbling Jerusalem)

Thursday of the First Week of Advent: 3:13—4:1 (judgment)

Friday of the First Week of Advent: Isa 5:8–16 (unjust)

Saturday of the First Week of Advent: Isa 5:17–30 (woe, invasion)

Second Sunday of Advent: 6:9–13 (prophet's mission)

Monday of the Second Week of Advent: 7:15–25 (Immanuel)

Tuesday of the Second Week of Advent: 8:1–9 (Isaiah's son)

Wednesday of the Second Week of Advent: Isa 8:11–20 (Isaiah's followers)

Thursday of the Second Week of Advent: Isa 9:7–20 (Northern Kingdom falls)

Friday of the Second Week of Advent: Isa 10:1–4, 8–12 (injustice)

Saturday of the Second Week of Advent: Isa 10:17–34 (fire of Israel; Sennacherib's invasion)

Third Sunday of Advent: Isa 11:11–12 (remnant)

Monday of the Third Week of Advent: Isa 13:1–11 (Babylon 1)

Tuesday of the Third Week of Advent: Isa 13:12–22 (Babylon 2)

Wednesday of the Third Week of Advent: Isa 14:1–11
(King of Babylon 1)

Thursday of the Third Week of Advent: Isa 14:12–23
(King of Babylon 2)

Friday of the Third Week of Advent: Isa 14:24–32 (Assyria)

Fourth Sunday of Advent: Isa 15:1–9 (Moab 1)

Dec. 17: Isa 16:1–13 (Moab 2)

Dec. 18: Isa 17:1–14 (Damascus)

Dec. 19: Isa 18:1–7 (Ethiopia)

Dec. 20: Isa 19:1–12 (Egypt 1)

Dec. 21: Isa 19:13–25 (Egypt 2)

Dec. 22: Isa 20:1–6 (captivity of Egypt and Ethiopia)

Dec. 23: Isa 21:1–10 (fall of Babylon)

Dec. 24: Isa 21:11–17 (Edom and Arabia)

Advent Alternative 2

First Sunday of Advent: Isa 22:1–14 (Jerusalem)

Monday of the First Week of Advent: Isa 22:15–18, 24–25
(Shebna and Eliakim)

Tuesday of the First Week of Advent: Isa 23:1–9 (Tyre and
Sidon 1)

Wednesday of the First Week of Advent: Isa 23:10–18
(Tyre and Sidon 2)

Thursday of the First Week of Advent: Isa 24:1–13 (devastation 1)

Friday of the First Week of Advent: Isa 24:14–23 (devastation 2)

Saturday of the First Week of Advent: Isa 25:1–5, 10b–12
  (devastation 3)

Second Sunday of Advent: Isa 26:10–11, 13–15, 20–21
  (devastation 4)

Monday of the Second Week of Advent: Isa 27:1–13
  (devastation 5)

Tuesday of the Second Week of Advent: Isa 28:1–6 (Samaria)

Wednesday of the Second Week of Advent: Isa 28:7–13 (Judah 1)

Thursday of the Second Week of Advent: Isa 28:14–29 (Judah 2)

Friday of the Second Week of Advent: Isa 29:1–16 (fall of
  Jerusalem)

Saturday of the Second Week of Advent: Isa 30:1–18 (futile
  alliance with Egypt 1)

Third Sunday of Advent: Isa 30:27–33 (Assyria judged)

Monday of the Third Week of Advent: Isa 31:1–9 (futile
  alliance with Egypt 2)

Tuesday of the Third Week of Advent: Isa 32:1–8 (justice)

Wednesday of the Third Week of Advent: Isa 32:9–14, 19–20
  (women of Jerusalem)

Thursday of the Third Week of Advent: Isa 33:1–16
  (Assyria overthrown)

Friday of the Third Week of Advent: Isa 33:17–24 (Zion restored)

Fourth Sunday of Advent: Isa 34:1–17 (Edom)

Dec. 17: Isa 36:1–22 (invasion of Sennacherib 1)

Dec. 18: Isa 37:1–20 (invasion of Sennacherib 2)

Dec. 19: Isa 37:21–32 (invasion of Sennacherib 3)

Dec. 20: Isa 37:33–38 (invasion of Sennacherib 4)

Dec. 21: Isa 38:9, 21–22 (Hezekiah's recovery 1)

Dec. 22: Isa 39:1–8 (Hezekiah's recovery 2)

Dec. 23: Isa 40:12–24 (Creator's power)

Dec. 24: Isa 41:1–5, 11–12 (Israel's liberator 1

Advent Alternative 3

First Sunday of Advent: Isa 41:21–29 (Israel's liberator 2)

Monday of the First Week of Advent: Isa 42:8–25 (salvation)

Tuesday of the First Week of Advent: Isa 43:1–15, 23–24, 26–28 (redemption and restoration)

Wednesday of the First Week of Advent: Isa 44:6–17 (the true God 1)

Thursday of the First Week of Advent: 44:18–23 (the true God 2)

Friday of the First Week of Advent: Isa 44:24–28; 45:2–3 (Cyrus)

Saturday of the First Week of Advent: Isa 45:9–17, 19–21a (woe)

Second Sunday of Advent: Isa 46:1–13 (Babylon's gods)

Monday of the Second Week of Advent: Isa 47:1–15 (Babylon falls)

Tuesday of the Second Week of Advent: Isa 48:1–9 (exiles 1)

Wednesday of the Second Week of Advent: Isa 48:10–16, 20–22 (exiles 2)

Thursday of the Second Week of Advent: Isa 49:7, 16–26 (redeemer 1)

Friday of the Second Week of Advent: Isa 50:1–3, 9b–11 (sins, crimes)

Saturday of the Second Week of Advent: Isa 51:1–13 (trust 1)

Third Sunday of Advent: Isa 51:14–23 (trust 2)

Monday of the Third Week of Advent: Isa 52:1–6, 11–12 (Zion 1)

Tuesday of the Third Week of Advent: Isa 54:15–17 (Zion 2)

Wednesday of the Third Week of Advent: Isa 56:3b–5, 9–12 (foreigners, blind shepherds)

Thursday of the Third Week of Advent: Isa 57:1–14, 20–21 (faithless)

Friday of the Third Week of Advent: Isa 59:1–15a (confession)

Fourth Sunday of Advent: Isa 59:15b–21 (redeemer 2)

Dec. 17: Isa 60:7–14 (flocks)

Dec. 18: Isa 60:15–22 (Zion 3)

Dec. 19: Isa 61:3c–5, 6b–8; 62:6–10 (reward)

Dec. 20: Isa 63:1–6, 10–15, 18–19 (Edom punished)

Dec. 21: Isa 64:1, 8–11 (anger)

Dec. 22: Isa 65:1–10 (rebels 1)

Dec. 23: Isa 65:11–16, 22–25 (rebels 2, renewal)

Dec. 24: Isa 66:1–9, 15–17, 22–24 (LORD's word, mother Zion, new heavens and new earth)

Advent Alternative 4

First Sunday of Advent: Gal 1:3–5 (greetings)

Monday of the First Week of Advent: Gal 2:3–6, 15, 17–18 (council)

Tuesday of the First Week of Advent: Gal 3:15–21 (law)

Wednesday of the First Week of Advent: Gal 4:1–3, 9–11 (freedom 1)

Thursday of the First Week of Advent: Gal 4:20–21, 25, 28–30
(freedom 2)

Friday of the First Week of Advent: Gal 5:7–12 (misled)

Saturday of the First Week of Advent: Gal 6:1–10
(life in community)

Second Sunday of Advent: Gal 6:11–13 (conclusion)

Monday of the Second Week of Advent: Eph 4:17–24
(speak truth 1)

Tuesday of the Second Week of Advent: Eph 4:25–29
(speak truth 2)

Wednesday of the Second Week of Advent: Eph 6:21–24 (news)

Thursday of the Second Week of Advent: Phil 1:12–18
(gospel advanced)

Friday of the Second Week of Advent: Phil 2:19–24 (Timothy)

Saturday of the Second Week of Advent: Phil 3:1–2, 15–16
(Beware! 1)

Third Sunday of Advent: Phil 4:2–3, 22–23 (Beware! 2)

Monday of the Third Week of Advent: Col 2:4–5, 16–23
(present in spirit)

Tuesday of the Third Week of Advent: Col 3:22, 25—4:6 (slaves)

Wednesday of the Third Week of Advent: Col 4:7–14
(greetings 1)

Thursday of the Third Week of Advent: Col 4:15–18 (greetings 2)

Friday of the Third Week of Advent: 1 Thess 1:6–8a, 14–20
(imitators)

Fourth Sunday of Advent: 1 Thess 3:1–6 (plans)

Dec. 17: : 1 Thess 5:7–8, 12–15 (vigilance)

Dec. 18: 2 Thess 1:6–10 (God's justice)

Dec. 19: 2 Thess 2:3b–13 (lawless)

Dec. 20: Thess 3:13–15 (do good)

Dec. 21: Titus 1:10–16 (rebels)

Dec. 22: Titus 2:9–10, 15 (slaves)

Dec. 23: Titus 3:8–15 (Titus)

Dec. 24: Phlm 1:1–6, 21–25 (address)

5

Christmas Alternative

with 2 John, 3 John, Jude,
1 Timothy, 2 Timothy

Because the current First Reading pericopes for Christmas are the same every year, what follows are alternative First Readings based on the principle of continuous or semi-continuous readings. In this Christmas scenario, the gospel passages found in the Lectionary are not altered; only the First Reading is altered. The following Christmas alternative can be considered an alternate set of First Readings for Christmas that can be used by individuals, assigned by the administration of a church, or left to the choice of a pastor of a parish. December 25 alternative texts can be found on page 181; December 26–28 are feasts.

December 29: Fifth Day in the Octave of Christmas: 2 John 1:1–3, 10–13 (Lady)

December 30: Sixth Day in the Octave of Christmas: 3 John 1:1–4, 9–12 (Gaius)

December 31: Seventh Day in the Octave of Christmas: Jude 1:1–7 (common salvation)

January 1: Solemnity of Mary, Mother of God: Jude 1:8–16, 18–19 (dreamers)

January 2: 1 Tim 1:3–11 (doctrine)

January 3: 1 Tim 1:18–20 (responsibility)

January 4: 1 Tim 2:9–15 (women)

January 5: 1 Tim 4:1–11 (asceticism)

January 6: 1 Tim 5:1–2, 11–25 (rules)

January 7: 1 Tim 6:1–2a (slaves)

Monday after Epiphany or January 7: 1 Tim 6:20–21 (Timothy)

Tuesday after Epiphany or January 8: 2 Tim 1:15–18 (Paul's suffering)

Wednesday after Epiphany or January 9: 2 Tim 2:4–7 (conduct)

Thursday after Epiphany or January 10: 2 Tim 2:16–26 (idle talk)

Friday after Epiphany or January 11: 2 Tim 3:1–7 (last days)

Saturday after Epiphany or January 12: 2 Tim 4:19–22 (greetings)

The *Lectionary* and the *Bible*

6

Lent Alternatives

(1) with Jeremiah 1:2—29:15

(2) with Jeremiah 29:16—52:34

(3) with Job

Because the current First Reading pericopes for Lent are the same every year, what follows are alternative First Readings based on the principle of continuous or semi-continuous readings. In this Lent scenario, the gospel passages found in the Lectionary are not altered; only the First Reading is altered. The following Lent alternatives can be considered alternate sets of First Readings for Lent that can be used by individuals, assigned by the administration of a church, or left to the choice of a pastor of a parish. The Second Reading on Sundays of Lent remains as in the Lectionary.

Lent Alternative 1

Ash Wednesday: Jer 1:2–3; 2:4–6, 9–11 (Jeremiah)

Thursday after Ash Wednesday: Jer 2:14–24 (unfaithful Israel 1)

Friday after Ash Wednesday: Jer 2:25–37 (unfaithful Israel 2)

Saturday after Ash Wednesday: Jer 3:1–13, 18 (unfaithful Israel 3)

First Sunday of Lent: Jer 3:19—4:4 (unfaithful Israel 4)

Monday of the First Week of Lent: Jer 4:5–18 (invasion from the North 1)

Tuesday of the First Week of Lent: Jer 4:19–31 (invasion from the North 2)

Wednesday of the First Week of Lent: Jer 5:1–13 (corrupt Jerusalem 1)

Thursday of the First Week of Lent: Jer 5:14–31 (corrupt Jerusalem 2)

Friday of the First Week of Lent: Jer 6:1–15 (enemy 1)

Saturday of the First Week of Lent: 6:16–30 (enemy 2)

Second Sunday of Lent: Jer 7:12–22 (temple sermon)

Monday of the Second Week of Lent: Jer 7:29–34; 8:1–3 9 (Judah rejected)

Tuesday of the Second Week of Lent: Jer 8:4–17 (Israel's conduct)

Wednesday of the Second Week of Lent: Jer 8:18–23 (Jeremiah's grief)

Thursday of the Second Week of Lent: Jer 9:1–15 (corruption)

Friday of the Second Week of Lent: Jer 9:16–25 (dirge)

Saturday of the Second Week of Lent: Jer 10:1–16 (idolatry)

Third Sunday of Lent: Jer 10:17–25 (Judah abandoned)

Monday of the Third Week of Lent: Jer 11:1–17
    (covenant fidelity)

Tuesday of the Third Week of Lent: Jer 12:1–23 (the way of
    the godless)

Wednesday of the Third Week of Lent: Jer 13:12–27 (wineflask)

Thursday of the Third Week of Lent: Jer 14:1–16 (drought)

Friday of the Third Week of Lent: Jer 15:1–9, 11, 15 (scourges)

Saturday of the Third Week of Lent: Jer 16:1–9 (Jeremiah's life 1)

Fourth Sunday of Lent: Jer 16:10–21 (Jeremiah's life 2)

Monday of the Fourth Week of Lent: Jer 17:1–4, 11–13
    (Judah's sin)

Tuesday of the Fourth Week of Lent: Jer 17:14–27 (vengeance)

Wednesday of the Fourth Week of Lent: Jer 18:7–17, 21–23
    (potter's vessel, Judah's apostasy)

Thursday of the Fourth Week of Lent: Jer 19:1–15 (potter's flask)

Friday of the Fourth Week of Lent: Jer 20:1–6, 14–18 (Pashhur,
    curses)

Saturday of the Fourth Week of Lent: Jer 21:1–10 (Zedekiah's
    fate 1)

Fifth Sunday of Lent: Jer 21:11–14; 22:1–9 (house of Judah)

Monday of the Fifth Week of Lent: Jer 22:10–30 (kings)

Tuesday of the Fifth Week of Lent: Jer 23:9–29 (false prophets 1)

Wednesday of the Fifth Week of Lent: Jer 23:30–40 (false prophets 2)

Thursday of the Fifth Week of Lent: Jer 24:1–10 (figs)

Friday of the Fifth Week of Lent: Jer 25:1–14 (exile)

Saturday of the Fifth Week of Lent: Jer 25:15–38 (cup)

Holy Week: Passion (Palm) Sunday: Jer 26:10, 17–23 (Jeremiah's life threatened)

Monday of Holy Week: Jer 27:1–11 (yoke 1)

Tuesday of Holy Week: Jer 27:12–22 (yoke 2)

Wednesday of Holy Week: Jer 29:1–15 (letter to exiles 1)

Lent Alternative 2

Ash Wednesday: Jer 29:16–32 (letter to exiles 2)

Thursday after Ash Wednesday: Jer 30:3–11, 16–17, 23–24 (restoration 1)

Friday after Ash Wednesday: Jer 31:15–20 (Rachel's mourning)

Saturday after Ash Wednesday: Jer 31:21–30, 38–40 (return)

First Sunday of Lent: Jer 32:1–23 (restoration 2)

Monday of the First Week of Lent: Jer 32:24–44 (restoration 3)

Tuesday of the First Week of Lent: Jer 33:1–13 (Jerusalem restored 1)

Wednesday of the First Week of Lent: Jer 33:17–26 (Jerusalem restored 2)

Thursday of the First Week of Lent: Jer 34:1–11 (Zedekiah's fate 2)

Friday of the First Week of Lent: Jer 34:12–22 (Zedekiah's fate 3)

Saturday of the First Week of Lent: 35:1–19 (Rechabites)

Second Sunday of Lent: Jer 36:1–19 (Baruch 1)

Monday of the Second Week of Lent: Jer 36:20–32 (Baruch 2)

Tuesday of the Second Week of Lent: Jer 37:1–10 (dungeon 1)

Wednesday of the Second Week of Lent: Jer 37:11–21 (dungeon 2)

Thursday of the Second Week of Lent: Jer 38:1–3, 7, 11–13 (cistern 1)

Friday of the Second Week of Lent: Jer 38:14–28 (cistern 2)

Saturday of the Second Week of Lent: Jer 39:1–18 (Gedaliah)

Third Sunday of Lent: Jer 40:1–16 (Jeremiah in chains)

Monday of the Third Week of Lent: Jer 41:1–10 (Gedaliah murdered)

Tuesday of the Third Week of Lent: Jer 41:11–18 (flight to Egypt)

Wednesday of the Third Week of Lent: 42:1–14 (prayer 1)

Thursday of the Third Week of Lent: Jer 42:15–22 (prayer 2)

Friday of the Third Week of Lent: Jer 43:1–13 (to Egypt)

Saturday of the Third Week of Lent: Jer 44:1–14 (Egypt 1)

Fourth Sunday of Lent: Jer 44:15–30 (Egypt 2)

Monday of the Fourth Week of Lent: Jer 45:1–5 (message to Baruch)

Tuesday of the Fourth Week of Lent: Jer 46:1–12 (against Egypt 1)

Wednesday of the Fourth Week of Lent: Jer 46:13–28 (against Egypt 2)

Thursday of the Fourth Week of Lent: Jer 47:1–7 (against the Philistines)

Friday of the Fourth Week of Lent: Jer 48:1–20 (against Moab 1)

Saturday of the Fourth Week of Lent: Jer 48:21–47 (against Moab 2)

Fifth Sunday of Lent: Jer 49:1–13 (against the Ammonites 1)

Monday of the Fifth Week of Lent: Jer 49:14–27 (against the Ammonites 2)

Tuesday of the Fifth Week of Lent: Jer 49:28–39 (against Arabia)

Wednesday of the Fifth Week of Lent: Jer 50:1–15 (against Babylon 1)

Thursday of the Fifth Week of Lent: Jer 50:16–30 (against Babylon 2)

Friday of the Fifth Week of Lent: Jer 50:31–46 (against Babylon 3)

Saturday of the Fifth Week of Lent: Jer 51:1–10 (against Babylon 4)

Holy Week: Passion (Palm) Sunday: Jer 51:11–19 or Jer 52:1–11 (against Babylon 5, Jerusalem captured)

Monday of Holy Week: Jer 51:20–32 or 52:12–16 (against Babylon 6, Jerusalem destroyed 1)

Tuesday of Holy Week: Jer 51:33–49 or Jer 52:17–27a (against Babylon 7, Jerusalem destroyed 2)

Wednesday of Holy Week: Jer 51:50–64 or Jer 52:27b–34 (against Babylon 8, exile)

Lent Alternative 3

Ash Wednesday: Job 1:1–5; 2:1–10 (wealth and piety)

Thursday after Ash Wednesday: Job 2:11–13 (Job's friends)

Friday after Ash Wednesday: Job 3:1–10, 18–19, 24–26 (Job's first speech)

Saturday after Ash Wednesday: Job 4:1–21 (Eliphaz's first speech 1)

First Sunday of Lent: Job 5:1–27 (Eliphaz's first speech 2)

Monday of the First Week of Lent: Job 6:1–30 (Job's first reply)

Tuesday of the First Week of Lent: Job 8:1–22 (Bildad's first speech)

Wednesday of the First Week of Lent: Job 9:1, 13, 17–35 (Job's second reply 1)

Thursday of the First Week of Lent: Job 10:1–22 (Job's second reply 2)

Friday of the First Week of Lent: Job 11:1–20 (Zophar's first speech)

Saturday of the First Week of Lent Job 12:1–25 (Job's third reply 1)

Second Sunday of Lent: Job 13:1–27 (Job's third reply 2)

Monday of the Second Week of Lent: Job 14:1–22 (Job's third reply 3)

Tuesday of the Second Week of Lent: Job 15:1–35 (Eliphaz's second speech)

Wednesday of the Second Week of Lent: Job 16:1–22 (Job's fourth reply 1)

Thursday of the Second Week of Lent: Job 17:1–16 (Job's fourth reply 2)

Friday of the Second Week of Lent: Job 18:1–21 (Bildad's second speech)

Saturday of the Second Week of Lent: Job 19:1–20, 26–29 (Job's fifth reply)

Third Sunday of Lent: Job 20:1–29 (Zophar's second speech)

Monday of the Third Week of Lent: Job 21:1–29 (Job's sixth reply)

Tuesday of the Third Week of Lent: Job 22:1–30 (Eliphaz's third speech)

Wednesday of the Third Week of Lent: Job 23:1–17
(Job's seventh reply 1)

Thursday of the Third Week of Lent: Job 24:1–25
(Job's seventh reply 2)

Friday of the Third Week of Lent: Job 25:1–6 (Bildad's
third speech)

Saturday of the Third Week of Lent: Job 26:1–14 (Job's
eighth reply 1)

Fourth Sunday of Lent: Job 27:1–21 (Job's eighth reply 2)

Monday of the Fourth Week of Lent: Job 28:1–28 (Job's
eighth reply 3)

Tuesday of the Fourth Week of Lent: Job 29:1–20 (Job's cause 1)

Wednesday of the Fourth Week of Lent: Job 30:1–31 (Job's cause 2)

Thursday of the Fourth Week of Lent: Job 31:1–15, 21–23, 26–30,
33–37 (Job's cause 3)

Friday of the Fourth Week of Lent: Job 32:1–22 (Elihu's speeches 1)

Saturday of the Fourth Week of Lent: Job 33:1–33 (Elihu's
speeches 2

Fifth Sunday of Lent: Job 34:1–37 (Elihu's speeches 3)

Monday of the Fifth Week of Lent: Job 35:1–16 (Elihu's speeches 4)

Tuesday of the Fifth Week of Lent: Job 36:1–22 (Elihu's speeches 5)

Wednesday of the Fifth Week of Lent: Job 37:1–24 (Elihu's
speeches 6)

Thursday of the Fifth Week of Lent: Job 38:1–7, 22–41 (the
LORD's speeches 1)

Friday of the Fifth Week of Lent: Job 38:1; 39:1–18 (the LORD's
speeches 2)

Saturday of the Fifth Week of Lent: Job 38:1; 39:19–30 (the LORD's speeches 3)

Holy Week: Passion (Palm) Sunday: Job 40:1–2, 6–18 (the LORD's speeches 4)

Monday of Holy Week: Job 40:6, 19–32 (the LORD's speeches 5)

Tuesday of Holy Week: 40:6, 15; 41:1–26 (the LORD's speeches 6)

Wednesday of Holy Week: Job 42:7–11, 17 (the LORD's speeches 7)

7

Easter Alternatives

(1) with Revelation, Hebrews, James, 1 Peter, 2 Peter

(2) with Acts

Because the current First Reading pericopes for Easter are the same every year, what follows are alternative First Readings based on the principle of continuous or semi-continuous readings. In this Easter scenario, the gospel passages found in the Lectionary are not altered; only the First Reading is altered. The following Easter alternative can be considered an alternate set of First Readings for Easter that can be used by individuals, assigned by the administration of a church, or left to the choice of a pastor of a parish. The Second Reading on Sundays of Easter remains as in the Lectionary.

Easter Alternative 1

Monday of the Octave of Easter: Rev 1:14–16, 20 (first and last)

Tuesday of the Octave of Easter: Rev 2:5–8 (Ephesus)

Wednesday of the Octave of Easter: Rev 2:12–17 (Pergamum)

Thursday of the Octave of Easter: Rev 2:18–29 (Thyatira)

Friday of the Octave of Easter: Rev 3:7–13 (Philadelphia)

Saturday of the Octave of Easter: Rev 5:13–14 (worship)

Second Sunday of Easter: Rev 6:1—7:1, 5–8 (seals)

Monday of Easter 2: Rev 8:1–2 (trumpets 1)

Tuesday of Easter 2: Rev 8:5–13 (trumpets 2)

Wednesday of Easter 2: Rev 9:1–12 (trumpets 3)

Thursday of Easter 2: Rev 9:13–21 (trumpets 4)

Friday of Easter 2: Rev 10:1–7 (small scroll)

Saturday of Easter 2: Rev 11:1–3, 13–14 (two witnesses)

Third Sunday of Easter: Rev 11:15–19a (trumpets 5)

Monday of Easter 3: Rev 12:12b–18 (dragon)

Tuesday of Easter 3: Rev 13:1–10 (beast 1)

Wednesday of Easter 3: Rev 13:11–18 (beast 2)

Thursday of Easter 3: Rev 14:6–12 (three angels)

Friday of Easter 3: Rev 15:5–8 (seven angels)

Saturday of Easter 3: Rev 16:1–21 (seven bowls)

Fourth Sunday of Easter: Rev 17:1–18 (Babylon 1)

Monday of Easter 4: Rev 18:3–20, 24 (Babylon 2)

Tuesday of Easter 4: Rev 19:9b–21 (king of kings)

Wednesday of Easter 4: Rev 20:5–10; 21:8 (dead)

Thursday of Easter 4: Rev 21:15–21, 24–26 (city measurements)

Friday of Easter 4: Rev 22:8–11, 15, 18–19 (attestation)

Saturday of Easter 4: Heb 1:7–14 (angel and Son)

Fifth Sunday of Easter: Heb 2:1–4 (faithfulness)

Monday of Easter 5: Heb 3:1–6 (Jesus vs. Moses)

Tuesday of Easter 5: Heb 3:15–19; 4:6–10 (rebels, rest)

Wednesday of Easter 5: Heb 5:11—6:9 (renewal)

Thursday of Easter 5: Heb 7:4–14, 18–24 (Melchizedek)

Friday of Easter 5: Heb 9:1, 4–10, 16–23 (worship regulations)

Saturday of Easter 5: Heb 10:26–31 (sin)

Sixth Sunday of Easter: Heb 11:20–31 (Isaac, Moses)

Monday of Easter 6: Heb 12:12, 16–17, 25–29 (lessons)

Tuesday of Easter 6: Heb 13:22–25 (exhortation)

Wednesday of Easter 6: Jas 2:10–13 (law)

Thursday of Easter 6: Jas 3:10–12 (tongue)

Friday of Easter 6: Jas 4:11–12 (speaking evil)

Saturday of Easter 6: 1 Pet 1:1–2 (greetings)

Seventh Sunday of Easter: 1 Pet 2:11–19 (citizen, slaves)

Monday of Easter 7: 1 Pet 3:10–13; 4:1–6 (conduct)

Tuesday of Easter 7: 2 Pet 1:1, 8–15 (greetings)

Wednesday of Easter 7: 2 Pet 1:20–21; 2:1–10a (prophecy)

Thursday of Easter 7: 2 Pet 2:10b–22 (false teachers)

Friday of Easter 7: 2 Pet 3:1–7 (parousia)

Saturday of Easter 7: 2 Pet 3:16 (Paul hard to understand)

Easter Alternative 2

Monday of the Octave of Easter: Acts 1:15–19; 2:12–13
  (Matthias, Pentecost)

Tuesday of the Octave of Easter: Act 2:15–21 (Peter's speech)

Wednesday of the Octave of Easter: Acts 5:1–11
  (Ananias and Saphira)

Thursday of the Octave of Easter: Acts 7:1–8
  (Stephen's discourse 1)

Friday of the Octave of Easter: Acts 7:9–16
  (Stephen's discourse 2)

Saturday of the Octave of Easter: 7:17–29 (Stephen's discourse 3)

Second Sunday of Easter: Acts 7:30–43 (Stephen's discourse 4)

Monday of Easter 2: Acts 8:9–13, 18–25 (Simon the magician)

Tuesday of Easter 2: Acts 9:23–25 (Saul escapes the Jews)

Wednesday of Easter 2: Acts 10:1–24 (Cornelius' vision 1)

Thursday of Easter 2: Acts 10:27–32 (Cornelius' vision 2)

Friday of Easter 2: Acts 12:12–19 (Rhoda)

Saturday of Easter 2: Acts 12:20–23 (Herod's death)

Third Sunday of Easter: Acts 13:5–12 (Mission: Barnabas
  and Saul 1)

Monday of Easter 3: Acts 14:1–4; 15:32-35 (Mission: Barnabas and Saul 2)

Tuesday of Easter 3: Acts 15:36–41 (Barnabas and Saul separate)

Wednesday of Easter 3: Acts 16:16–21, 35–40 (Philippi)

Thursday of Easter 3: Acts 17:1–14 (Thessalonica)

Friday of Easter 3: Acts 17:16–21 (Athens)

Saturday of Easter 3: Acts 18:19–22; 19:9–20 (Ephesus, exorcists)

Fourth Sunday of Easter: Acts 19:21–27 (plans and silversmiths 1)

Monday of Easter 4: Acts 19:28–40 (silversmiths 2)

Tuesday of Easter 4: Acts 20:1–6 (Macedonia)

Wednesday of Easter 4: Acts 20:7–12 (Eutychus)

Thursday of Easter 4: Acts 20:13–16 (Miletus)

Friday of Easter 4: Acts 21:1–14 (Tyre)

Saturday of Easter 4: Acts 21:15–26 (Jerusalem)

Fifth Sunday of Easter: Acts 21:27–40 (Paul arrested)

Monday of Easter 5: Acts 22:1–2, 17–21 (Paul's defense)

Tuesday of Easter 5: Acts 22:22–29 (Paul inspired)

Wednesday of Easter 5: Acts 23:1–5 (Paul to the Sanhedrin)

Thursday of Easter 5: Acts 23:12–22 (Paul's transfer 1)

Friday of Easter 5: Acts 23:23–35 (Paul's transfer 2)

Saturday of Easter 5: Acts 24:1–15 (Felix 1)

Sixth Sunday of Easter: Acts 24:16–27 (Felix 2)

Monday of Easter 6: Acts 25:1–12 (Festus)

Tuesday of Easter 6: Acts 25:22–27 (Agrippa 1)

Wednesday of Easter 6: Acts 26:1–11 (Agrippa 2)

Thursday of Easter 6: Acts 26:12–18 (Agrippa 3)

Friday of Easter 6: Acts 26:24–32 (reaction to Paul's speech)

Saturday of Easter 6: Acts 27:1–5 (Paul's departure for Rome)

Seventh Sunday of Easter: Acts 27:6–12 (shipwreck)

Monday of Easter 7: Acts 27:13–20 (winter)

Tuesday of Easter 7: Acts 27:21–32 (courage)

Wednesday of Easter 7: Acts 27:33–38 (eat)

Thursday of Easter 7: Acts 27:39–44 (beach)

Friday of Easter 7: Acts 28:1–7 (Malta)

Saturday of Easter 7: Acts 28:21–28 (Paul in Rome)

The *Lectionary* and the *Bible*

8

Ordinary Time Alternatives

(1) with Wisdom, Sirach, Proverbs, Ecclesiastes, Song of Songs, Daniel, Joel, Habakkuk

(2) with Ezekiel, Amos, Micah, Nahum, Zephaniah, Haggai, Zechariah, Lamentations, Baruch, 1 Chronicles

(3) with 2 Chronicles, Ezra, Nehemiah, Tobit, 1 Maccabees, 2 Maccabees

(4) with Genesis, Exodus, Leviticus, Numbers 9:14

(5) with Numbers 9:1, Deuteronomy, Joshua, Judges, Ruth

(6) with 1 Samuel, 2 Samuel, 1 Kings, 2 Kings, 2 Chr 36 or Ezra 1–2

What follows are thirty-four-week alternatives of First Readings based on the principle of continuous or semi-continuous readings. In these scenarios, the gospel passages found in the Lectionary are not altered; only the First Reading is changed. The following alternatives can be considered alternate sets of First Readings for Ordinary Time Sunday Cycles A, B, or C and Weekday Year I or II that can be used by individuals, assigned by the administration of a church, or left to the choice of a pastor of a parish. The Second Reading on Sundays of Ordinary Time remains as in the Lectionary.

Ordinary Time Alternative 1

Monday of Week 1: Wis 1:8–12 (justice)

Tuesday of Week 1: Wis 1:16; 2:1b–11 (death)

Wednesday of Week 1: Wis 3:10–19 (the wicked)

Thursday of Week 1: Wis 4:1–6 (children)

Friday of Week 1: Wis 4:16–19 (dead just man)

Saturday of Week 1: Wis 4:20—5:12 (judgment of wicked 1)

Second Sunday in Ordinary Time: Wis 5:13-23
(judgment of wicked 2)

Monday of Week 2: Wis 6:17–25 (discipline)

Tuesday of Week 2: Wis 7:1-6, 11–14, 17–21 (mortal man)

Wednesday of Week 2: Wis 8:2–16 (wisdom sought)

Thursday of Week 2: Wis 8:17–21 (wisdom gift)

Friday of Week 2: Wis 9:1–8, 12 (Solomon's prayer)

Saturday of Week 2: Wis 10:1–12 (wisdom's works 1)

Third Sunday in Ordinary Time: Wis 10:13–21; 11:1
(wisdom's works 2)

Monday of Week 3: Wis 11:2–14 (God's providence 1)

Tuesday of Week 3: Wis 11:15–21 (God's providence 2)

Wednesday of Week 3: Wis 12:3–12, 14–15, 20–22
    (God's providence 3)

Thursday of Week 3: Wis 12:23–27 (God's providence 4)

Friday of Week 3: Wis 13:10–19 (idols 1)

Saturday of Week 3: Wis 14:1–11 (idols 2)

Fourth Sunday in Ordinary Time: Wis 14:12–20 (idols 3)

Monday of Week 4: Wis 14:21–31 (idols 4)

Tuesday of Week 4: Wis 15:1–6 (belonging to God)

Wednesday of Week 4: Wis 15:7–19 (idols 5)

Thursday of Week 4: Wis 16:1–15 (idols 6)

Friday of Week 4: Wis 16:16–29 (God's providence 5)

Saturday of Week 4: Wis 17:1–10 (God's providence 6)

Fifth Sunday in Ordinary Time: Wis 17:11–21
    (God's providence 7)

Monday of Week 5: Wis 18:1–5, 10–13 (God's providence 8)

Tuesday of Week 5: Wis 18:17–25 (God's providence 9)

Wednesday of Week 5: Wis 19:1–5 (God's providence 10)

Thursday of Week 5: Wis 19:10–22 (God's providence 11)

Friday of Week 5: Sir 1:11–29 (wisdom's source)

Saturday of Week 5: Sir 2:14–18 (hope)

Sixth Sunday in Ordinary Time: Sir 3:1–2, 8–13, 27–28 (parents)

Monday of Week 6: Sir 3:29; 4:1–11 (the poor)

Tuesday of Week 6: Sir 4:23–31 (practice wisdom)

Wednesday of Week 6: Sir 5:11–17 (speech 1)

Thursday of Week 6: Sir 6:1–4 (speech 2)

Friday of Week 6: Sir 6:18–31(wisdom's blessings 1)

Saturday of Week 6: Sir 6:32–37 (wisdom's blessings 2)

Seventh Sunday in Ordinary Time: Sir 7:1–17 (public life 1)

Monday of Week 7: Sir 7:18–36 (public life 2)

Tuesday of Week 7: Sir 8:1-10 (prudence 1)

Wednesday of Week 7: Sir 8:11–19 (prudence 2)

Thursday of Week 7: Sir 9:1–9 (women 1)

Friday of Week 7: Sir 9:10–18 (friends 1)

Saturday of Week 7: Sir 10:1–18 (rulers 1)

Eighth Sunday in Ordinary Time: Sir 10:19–30 (glory)

Monday of Week 8: Sir 11:1–19 (poor man's wisdom)

Tuesday of Week 8: Sir 11:20–34 (duty)

Wednesday of Week 8: Sir 12:1–9 (do good 1)

Thursday of Week 8: Sir 12:10–18 (do good 2)

Friday of Week 8: Sir 13:1–13 (associates 1)

Saturday of Week 8: Sir 13:14–25 (associates 2)

Ninth Sunday in Ordinary Time: Sir 14:1–16 (happiness 1)

Monday of Week 9: Sir 14:17–27 (happiness 2)

Tuesday of Week 9: Sir 15:7–15 (fear the LORD)

Wednesday of Week 9: Sir 16:1–14 (sinners)

Thursday of Week 9: Sir 16:15–28 (not hidden from God)

Friday of Week 9: Sir 17:14–19 (rulers 2)

Saturday of Week 9: Sir 18:1–13 (God's power and mercy)

Tenth Sunday in Ordinary Time: Sir 18:14–33 (prudence 3)

Monday of Week 10: Sir 19:1–16 (prudence 4)

Tuesday of Week 10: Sir 19:17–29 (true wisdom)

Wednesday of Week 10: Sir 20:1–16 (wise vs. foolish 1)

Thursday of Week 10: Sir 20:17–30 (wise vs. foolish 2)

Friday of Week 10: Sir 21:1–10 (sin)

Saturday of Week 10: Sir 21:11–28 (wise vs. foolish 3)

Eleventh Sunday in Ordinary Time: Sir 22:1–11 (laziness and foolishness 1)

Monday of Week 11: Sir 22:12–18 (laziness and foolishness 2)

Tuesday of Week 11: Sir 22:19–26 (friendship)

Wednesday of Week 11: Sir 22:27—23:6 (prayer)

Thursday of Week 11: Sir 23:7–15 (the tongue 1)

Friday of Week 11: Sir 23:16–21 (sins)

Saturday of Week 11: Sir 23:22–27 (sins 2)

Twelfth Sunday in Ordinary Time: Sir 24:8–11, 17–25, 31 (wisdom praised)

Monday of Week 12: Sir 25:1–11 (praiseworthy)

Tuesday of Week 12: Sir 25:12–25 (women 2)

Wednesday of Week 12: Sir 26:5–15 (good wife)

Thursday of Week 12: Sir 27:1–4, 9–21 (sins 3)

Friday of Week 12: Sir 27:22–30; 28:10–11 (sins 4)

Saturday of Week 12: Sir 28:12–26 (the tongue 2)

Thirteenth Sunday in Ordinary Time: Sir 29:1–9 (loans, alms, and surety 1)

Monday of Week 13: Sir 29:10–20 (loams, alms, and surety 2)

Tuesday of Week 13: Sir 29:21–28 (frugality)

Wednesday of Week 13: Sir 30:1–13 (training children)

Thursday of Week 13: Sir 30:14–25 (health)

Friday of Week 13: Sir 31:1–11 (riches)

Saturday of Week 13: Sir 31:12–31 (table etiquette 1)

Fourteenth Sunday in Ordinary Time: Sir 32:1–13 (table etiquette 2)

Monday of Week 14: Sir 32:14–24 (God's providence)

Tuesday of Week 14: Sir 33:1–18 (fear the LORD)

Wednesday of Week 14: Sir 33:19–33 (dominion)

Thursday of Week 14: Sir 34:1–12 (trust in God 1)

Friday of Week 14: Sir 34:13–26 (trust in God 2)

Saturday of Week 14: Sir 35:18–19, 23–24 (keep Torah)

Fifteenth Sunday in Ordinary Time: Sir 36:3–4, 7–12 (prayer)

Monday of Week 15: Sir 36:20–27 (associates)

Tuesday of Week 15: Sir 37:1–15 (friends 2)

Wednesday of Week 15: Sir 37:16–30 (temperance)

Thursday of Week 15: Sir 38:1–23 (sickness and death)

Friday of Week 15: Sir 38:24–34 (craftsmen and scribes)

Saturday of Week 15: Sir 39:2–4, 15–35 (study the law)

Sixteenth Sunday in Ordinary Time: Sir 40:1–17a (life 1)

Monday of Week 16: Sir 40: 17b–30 (life 2)

Tuesday of Week 16: Sir 41:1–13 (life 3)

Wednesday of Week 16: Sir 41:14–24 (shame 1)

Thursday of Week 16: Sir 42:1–14 (shame 2)

Friday of Week 16: Sir 43:1–12 (nature 1)

Saturday of Week 16: Sir 43:13–35 (nature 2)

Seventeenth Sunday in Ordinary Time: Sir 44:2–8, 16–23
(ancestors 1)

Monday of Week 17: Sir 45:1–17 (ancestors 2)

Tuesday of Week 17: Sir 45:18–26 (ancestors 3)

Wednesday of Week 17: Sir 46:1–10 (ancestors 4)

Thursday of Week 17: Sir 46:11–20 (ancestors 5)

Friday of Week 17: Sir 47:1, 14–24a (ancestors 6)

Saturday of Week 17: Sir 47:24b–25; 48:16–25 (ancestors 7)

Eighteenth Sunday in Ordinary Time: Sir 49:1–13 (ancestors 8)

Monday of Week 18: Sir 49:14—50:11 (ancestors 9)

Tuesday of Week 18: Sir 50:12--23 (ancestors 10)

Wednesday of Week 18: Sir 50:27–29; 51:28–30 (wise instruction)

Thursday of Week 18: Prov 1:1–14 (purpose of proverbs 1)

Friday of Week 18: Prov 1:15–33 (purpose of proverbs 2)

Saturday of Week 18: Prov 2:10–22 (wisdom 1)

Nineteenth Sunday in Ordinary Time: Prov 3:1–26
(trust the LORD)

Monday of Week 19: Prov 4:1–6, 14–27 (wisdom as guide)

Tuesday of Week 19: Prov 5:1–14 (adultery)

Wednesday of Week 19: Prov 5:15–23 (drink from own cistern)

Thursday of Week 19: Prov 6:1–15 (miscellaneous proverbs 1)

Friday of Week 19: Prov 6:16–35 (miscellaneous proverbs 2)

Saturday of Week 19: Prov 7:1–13 (miscellaneous proverbs 3)

Twentieth Sunday in Ordinary Time: Prov 7:14–27
    (miscellaneous proverbs 4)

Monday of Week 20: Prov 8:1–21 (wisdom 2)

Tuesday of Week 20: Prov 8:24–27, 32–36 (wisdom 3)

Wednesday of Week 20: Prov 9:7–18 (wisdom 4)

Thursday of Week 20: Prov 10:1–16 (Solomon's proverbs 1)

Friday of Week 20: Prov 10:17–32 (Solomon's proverbs 2)

Saturday of Week 20: Prov 11:1–16 (Solomon's proverbs 3)

Twenty-first Sunday in Ordinary Time: Prov 11:17–31
    (Solomon's proverbs 4)

Monday of Week 21: Prov 12:1–14 (Solomon's proverbs 5)

Tuesday of Week 21: Prov 12:15–28 (Solomon's proverbs 6)

Wednesday of Week 21: Prov 13:1–12 (Solomon's proverbs 7)

Thursday of Week 21: Prov 13:13–25 (Solomon's proverbs 8)

Friday of Week 21 Prov 14:1–17 (Solomon's proverbs 9)

Saturday of Week 21: Prov 14:18–35 (Solomon's proverbs 10)

Twenty-second Sunday in Ordinary Time: Prov 15:1–17
    (Solomon's proverbs 11)

Monday of Week 22: Prov 15:18–33 (Solomon's proverbs 12)

Tuesday of Week 22: Prov 16:1–17 (Solomon's proverbs 13)

Wednesday of Week 22: Prov 16:18–33 (Solomon's proverbs 14)

Thursday of Week 22: Prov 17:1–14 (Solomon's proverbs 15)

Friday of Week 22: Prov 17:15–28 (Solomon's proverbs 16)

Saturday of Week 22: Prov 18:1–12 (Solomon's proverbs 17)

Twenty-third Sunday in Ordinary Time: Prov 18:13–24 (Solomon's proverbs 18)

Monday of Week 23: Prov 19:1–15 (Solomon's proverbs 19)

Tuesday of Week 23: Prov 19:16–29 (Solomon's proverbs 20)

Wednesday of Week 23: Prov 20:1–15 (Solomon's proverbs 21)

Thursday of Week 23: Prov 20:16–30 (Solomon's proverbs 22)

Friday of Week 23: Prov 21:7–9, 14–31 (Solomon's proverbs 23)

Saturday of Week 23: Prov 22:1–15 (Solomon's proverbs 24)

Twenty-fourth Sunday in Ordinary Time: Prov. 22:16–29 (Solomon's proverbs 25)

Monday of Week 24: Prov 23:1–18 (Solomon's proverbs 26)

Tuesday of Week 24: Prov 23:19–35 (Solomon's proverbs 27)

Wednesday of Week 24: Prov 24:1–22 (Solomon's proverbs 28)

Thursday of Week 24: Prov 24:23–34 (wise sayings)

Friday of Week 24: Prov 25:1–14 (Solomon's proverbs 29)

Saturday of Week 24: Prov 25:15–28 (Solomon's proverbs 30)

Twenty-fifth Sunday in Ordinary Time: Prov 26:1–14 (Solomon's proverbs 31)

Monday of Week 25: Prov 26:15–28 (Solomon's proverbs 32)

Tuesday of Week 25: Prov 27:1–14 (Solomon's proverbs 33)

Wednesday of Week 25: Prov 27:15–27 (Solomon's proverbs 34)

Thursday of Week 25: Prov 28:1–14 (Solomon's proverbs 35)

Friday of Week 25: Prov 28:15–28 (Solomon's proverbs 36)

Saturday of Week 25: Prov 29:1–14 (Solomon's proverbs 37)

Twenty-sixth Sunday in Ordinary Time: Prov 29:15–27 (Solomon's proverbs 38)

Monday of Week 26: Prov 30:1–4, 10–33 (words of Agur)

Tuesday of Week 26: Prov 31:1–9, 14–18, 21–29 (words of Lemuel)

Wednesday of Week 26: Eccl 1:1, 12–18; 2:24–26 (words of Qoheleth 1)

Thursday of Week 26: Eccl 3:12–22 (words of Qoheleth 2)

Friday of Week 26: Eccl 4:1–18 (words of Qoheleth 3)

Saturday of Week 26: Eccl 5:1–19 (words of Qoheleth 4)

Twenty-seventh Sunday in Ordinary Time: Eccl 6:1–12 (words of Qoheleth 5)

Monday of Week 27: Eccl 7:1–12 (words of Qoheleth 6)

Tuesday of Week 27: Eccl 7:13–29 (words of Qoheleth 7)

Wednesday of Week 27: Eccl 8:1–17 (words of Qoheleth 8)

Thursday of Week 27: Eccl 9:1–18 (words of Qoheleth 9)

Friday of Week 27: Eccl 10:1–10 (words of Qoheleth 10)

Saturday of Week 27: Eccl 10:11–20 (words of Qoheleth 11)

Twenty-eighth Sunday in Ordinary Time: Eccl 11:1–8 (words of Qoheleth 12)

Monday of Week 28: Eccl 12:9–14 (words of Qoheleth 13)

Tuesday of Week 28: Song 1:1–17 (love)

Wednesday of Week 28: Song 2:1–7, 15, 17 (flower)

Thursday of Week 28: Song 3:4b–11 (bridegroom)

Friday of Week 28: Song 4:1-8 (the beloved 1)

Saturday of Week 28: Song 4:9–16a (the beloved 2)

Twenty-ninth Sunday in Ordinary Time: Song 4:16b—5:8 (garden)

Monday of Week 29: Song 5:9–16 (lost love)

Tuesday of Week 29: Song 6:1–7 (lover in the garden 1)

Wednesday of Week 29: Song 6:8–12 (lover in the garden 2)

Thursday of Week 29: Song 7:1–6 (the bride)

Friday of Week 29: Song 7:7–10a (love's desires)

Saturday of Week 29: Song 7:10b–14 (love's union 1)

Thirtieth Sunday in Ordinary Time: Song 8:1–5 (love's union 2, homecoming)

Monday of Week 30: Song 8:8–10 (welcome)

Tuesday of Week 30: Song 8:11–14 (vineyard)

Wednesday of Week 30: Dan 2:1–13 (dream 1)

Thursday of Week 30: Dan 2:14–30 (dream 2)

Friday of Week 30: Dan 2:46–49 (dream 3)

Saturday of Week 30: Dan 3:1–13 (fiery furnace 1)

Thirtieth-first Sunday in Ordinary Time: Dan 3:21–33, 44–45 (fiery furnace 2)

Monday of Week 31: Dan 3:46–51, 89–90, 93–94, 96–97 (fiery furnace 3)

Tuesday of Week 31: Dan 3:98–100 (great tree)

Wednesday of Week 31: Dan 4:1–15 (another dream 1)

Thursday of Week 31: Dan 4:16–34 (another dream 2)

Friday of Week 31: Dan 5:7–12, 18–22, 29 (writing on the wall)

Saturday of Week 31: Dan 6:1–11, 29 (lions' den)

Thirty-second Sunday in Ordinary Time: Dan 7:1, 28: 8:1–12 (four beasts, ram and he-goat 1)

Monday of Week 32: Dan 8:13–27 (ram and he-goat 2)

Tuesday of Week 32: Dan 9:1–3, 11–27 (Gabriel)

Wednesday of Week 32: Dan 10:1–9 (war 1)

Thursday of Week 32: Dan 10:10—11:2a (war 2)

Friday of Week 32: Dan 11:2b–35 (war 3)

Saturday of Week 32: Dan 11: 36–45 (war 4)

Thirty-third Sunday in Ordinary Time: Dan 12:4–13 (secret)

Monday of Week 33: Dan 14:1–22 (Bel and the dragon 1)

Tuesday of Week 33 Dan 14:23–42 (Bell and the dragon 2)

Wednesday of Week 33: Joel 1:–12 (invasion)

Thursday of Week 33: Joel 1:16–20 (no food)

Friday of Week 33: Joel 2:3–11 (day of the Lord)

Saturday of Week 33: Joel 2:19–20, 25 (blessings)

Solemnity of Christ the King (Thirty-fourth Sunday in Ordinary Time): Joel 4:1–11 (restoration)

Monday of Week 34: Obad 1:1–9 (Edom 1)

Tuesday of Week 34: Obad 1:10–21 (Edom 2)

Wednesday of Week 34: Hab 1:1, 4–11 (Chaldea 1)

Thursday of Week 34: Hab 2:5–20 (Chaldea 2)

Friday of Week 34: Hab 3:1–11 (prayer 1)

Saturday of Week 34: Hab 3:12–19 (prayer 2)

Ordinary Time Alternative 2

Monday of Week 1: Ezek 1:1, 6–23, 28b (vision of God)

Tuesday of Week 1: Ezek 2:1, 6–7; 3:5–15 (scroll eating)

Wednesday of Week 1: Ezek 3:22–27 (dumbness)

Thursday of Week 1: Ezek 4:1–15 (siege and exile 1)

Friday of Week 1: Ezek 5:1–15 (siege and exile 2)

Saturday of Week 1: Ezek 6:1–14 (mountains of Israel)

Second Sunday in Ordinary Time: Ezek 7:1–14 (the end 1)

Monday of Week 2: Ezek 7:15–27 (the end 2)

Tuesday of Week 2: Ezek 8:1–13 (abomination 1)

Wednesday of Week 2: Ezek 8:14–18 (abomination 2)

Thursday of Week 2: Ezek 9:8–9, 24–25 (idolators slaughtered)

Friday of Week 2: Ezek 10:1–8 (glory leaves Jerusalem 1)

Saturday of Week 2: Ezek 10:9–17 (glory leaves Jerusalem 2)

Third Sunday in Ordinary Time: Ezek 11:1–12 (princes judged 1)

Monday of Week 3: Ezek 11:13–21 (princes judged 2)

Tuesday of Week 3: Ezek 12:13–28 (exile)

Wednesday of Week 3: Ezek 13:1–12 (against peace 1)

Thursday of Week 3: Ezek 13:13–21 (against peace 2)

Friday of Week 3: Ezek 14:1–11 (against idolators)

Saturday of Week 3: Ezek 14:12–23 (personal responsibility)

Fourth Sunday in Ordinary Time: Ezek 15:1–8 (vine parable)

Monday of Week 4: Ezek 16:16–29 (faithless spouse 1)

Tuesday of Week 4: Ezek 16:30–43 (faithless spouse 2)

Wednesday of Week 4: Ezek 16:44–58 (faithless spouse 3)

Thursday of Week 4: Ezek 17:1–10 (eagles and vine 1)

Friday of Week 4: Ezek 17:11–21 (eagles and vine 2)

Saturday of Week 4: Ezek 18:10–13a, 14–20 (responsibility)

Fifth Sunday in Ordinary Time: Ezek 19:1–9 (lamentation 1)

Monday of Week 5: Ezek 19:10–14 (lamentation 2)

Tuesday of Week 5: Ezek 20:1–17 (infidelity history 1)

Wednesday of Week 5: Ezek 20:18–38 (infidelity history 2)

Thursday of Week 5: Ezek 20:39–44 (infidelity history 3)

Friday of Week 5: Ezek 21:1–10 (sword 1)

Saturday of Week 5: Ezek 21:11–22 (sword 2)

Sixth Sunday in Ordinary Time: Ezek 21:23–37 (sword 3)

Monday of Week 6: Ezek 22:1–12 (Jerusalem's crimes 1)

Tuesday of Week 6: Ezek 22:13–22 (Jerusalem's crimes 2)

Wednesday of Week 6: Ezek 22:23–31 (Jerusalem's crimes 3)

Thursday of Week 6: Ezek 23:1–20 (two sisters 1)

Friday of Week 6: Ezek 23:21–34 (two sisters 2)

Saturday of Week 6: Ezek 23:35–49 (two sisters 3)

Seventh Sunday in Ordinary Time: Ezek 24:1–14 (the pot)

Monday of Week 7: Ezek 24:25–27 (end of Ezekiel's dumbness)

Tuesday of Week 7: Ezek 25:1–7 (against Ammon)

Wednesday of Week 7: Ezek 25:8–17 (against Moab, Edom, Philistia)

Thursday of Week 7: Ezek 26:1–14 (against Tyre 1)

Friday of Week 7: Ezek 26:15–21 (against Tyre 2)

Saturday of Week 7: Ezek 27:1–9 (Tyre ship 1)

Eighth Sunday in Ordinary Time: Ezek 27:10–27a (Tyre ship 2)

Monday of Week 8: Ezek 27:27b–36 (Tyre ship 3)

Tuesday of Week 8: Ezek 28:11–19 (lament for Tyre)

Wednesday of Week 8: Ezek 28:20–26 (against Sidon)

Thursday of Week 8: Ezek 29:1–9a (crocodile Egypt 1)

Friday of Week 8: Ezek 29:9b–21 (crocodile Egypt 2)

Saturday of Week 8: Ezek 30:1–12 (day of the LORD 1)

Ninth Sunday in Ordinary Time: Ezek 30:13–26
    (day of the LORD 2)

Monday of Week 9: Ezek 31:1–9 (cypress allegory 1)

Tuesday of Week 9: Ezek 31:10–18 (cypress allegory 2)

Wednesday of Week 9: Ezek 32:1–16 (dirge: pharaoh)

Thursday of Week 9: Ezek 32:17–32 (dirge: Egypt)

Friday of Week 9: Ezek 33:1–6 (watchmen)

Saturday of Week 9: Ezek 33:10–20 (retribution)

Tenth Sunday in Ordinary Time: Ezek 33:21–33 (survivors)

Monday of Week 10: Ezek 34:18–31 (shepherd)

Tuesday of Week 10: Ezek 35:1–15 (against Edom)

Wednesday of Week 10: Ezek 36:1–15 (land regenerated)

Thursday of Week 10: Ezek 36:29–38 (people regenerated)

Friday of Week 10: Ezek 38:1–16 (Gog 1)

Saturday of Week 10: Ezek 39:1–10 (Gog 2)

Eleventh Sunday in Ordinary Time: Ezek 39:11–20 (Gog 3)

Monday of Week 11: Ezek 39:21–29 (return)

Tuesday of Week 11: Ezek 40:1–16 (new temple 1)

Wednesday of Week 11: Ezek 40:17–27 (new temple 2)

Thursday of Week 11: Ezek 40:28–37 (new temple 3)

Friday of Week 11: Ezek 40:38–49 (new temple 4)

Saturday of Week 11: Ezek 41:1–15a (new temple 5)

Twelfth Sunday in Ordinary Time: Ezek 41:15b–26
(new temple 6)

Monday of Week 12: Ezek 42:1–10a (other structures 1)

Tuesday of Week 12: Ezek 42:10b–20 (other structures 2)

Wednesday of Week 12: Ezek 43:7b–12 (the LORD returns
to the temple)

Thursday of Week 12: Ezek 43:13–27 (altar)

Friday of Week 12: Ezek 44:1–9 (gate)

Saturday of Week 12: Ezek 44:10–14 (Levites)

Thirteenth Sunday in Ordinary Time: Ezek 44:15–31 (priests)

Monday of Week 13: Ezek 45:1–8 (tract of land)

Tuesday of Week 13: Ezek 45:9–17 (weights, measures, offerings)

Wednesday of Week Ezek 45:18–25 (Passover, Booths)

Thursday of Week 13: Ezek 46:1–15 (Sabbaths)

Friday of Week 13: Ezek 46:16–24 (prince, kitchen)

Saturday of Week 13: Ezek 47:13–23 (boundaries)

Fourteenth Sunday in Ordinary Time: Ezek 48:1–12 (tribes 1)

Monday of Week 14: Ezek 48:13–29 (tribes 2)

Tuesday of Week 14: Ezek 48:30–35 (gates)

Wednesday of Week 14: Amos 1:1–15 (nations judged 1)

Thursday of Week 14: Amos 2:1–5, 11–12 (nations judged 2)

Friday of Week 14: Amos 3:9–15 (Israel's woes 1)

Saturday of Week 14: Amos 4:1–10, 13 (Israel's woes 2)

Fifteenth Sunday in Ordinary Time: Amos 5:1–3, 5–13
    (Israel's woes 3)

Monday of Week 15: Amos 5:16–20, 25–27 (Israel's woes 4)

Tuesday of Week Amos 6:1b–3, 8–14 (Israel's woes 5)

Wednesday of Week 15: Amos 7:1–9 (locusts)

Thursday of Week 15: Amos 8:1–3, 7–8 (fruit basket)

Friday of Week 15: Amos 9:1–10 (altar)

Saturday of Week 15: Mic 1:1–7 (judgment 1)

Sixteenth Sunday in Ordinary Time: Mic 1:8–16 (judgment 2)

Monday of Week 16: Mic 2:6–13 (shame)

Tuesday of Week 16: Mic 3:1–6 (leaders fall 1)

Wednesday of Week 16: Mic 3:7–12 (leaders fall 2)

Thursday of Week 16: Mic 4:5–14 (walk with God)

Friday of Week 16: Mic 5:4b–14 (remnant)

Saturday of Week 16: Mic 6:5, 9–16 (remember)

Seventeenth Sunday in Ordinary Time: Mic 7:1–6
    (faithful gone 1)

Monday of Week 17: Mic 7:10–13, 16–17 (faithful gone 2)

Tuesday of Week 17: Nah:1–14 (Nineveh 1)

Wednesday of Week 17: Nah 2:4–14 (Nineveh 2)

Thursday of Week 17: Nah 3:4–5, 8–17 (Nineveh 3)

Friday of Week 17: Zeph 1:1–10 (day of the LORD 1)

Saturday of Week 17: Zeph 1:11—2:2 (day of the LORD 2)

Eighteenth Sunday in Ordinary Time: Zeph 2:14–15; 3:3–8 (Jerusalem)

Monday of Week 18: Hag 1:9–14 (rebuild the temple)

Tuesday of Week 18: Hag 2:10–19 (offerings)

Wednesday of Week 18: Hag 2:20–23 (Zerubbabel)

Thursday of Week 18: Zech 1:1–17 (conversion)

Friday of Week 18: Zech 2:1–4, 10–13 (four horns and blacksmiths)

Saturday of Week 18: Zech 3:1–10 (high priest)

Nineteenth Sunday in Ordinary Time: Zech 4:1–14 (interpretation)

Monday of Week 19: Zech 5:1–11 (flying scroll and bushel)

Tuesday of Week 19: Zech 6:1–15 (four chariots, shoot)

Wednesday of Week 19: Zech 7:1–14 (fasting)

Thursday of Week 19: Zech 8:9–19 (be strong!)

Friday of Week 19: Zech 9:1–8, 11–12 (the LORD comes 1)

Saturday of Week 19: Zech 9:13–17 (the LORD comes 2)

Twentieth Sunday in Ordinary Time: Zech 10:1–12 (new)

Monday of Week 20: Zech 11:1–17 (shepherds)

Tuesday of Week 20: Zech 12:1–9, 12–13 (Jerusalem)

Wednesday of Week 20: Zech 13:2–5, 8–9 (idols)

Thursday of Week 20: Zech 14:1–9 (nations vs. Jerusalem 1)

Friday of Week 20: Zech 14:10–21 (nations vs. Jerusalem 2)

Saturday of Week 20: Mal 1:1–5 (Israel)

Twenty-first Sunday in Ordinary Time: Mal 1:6–14
    (sins of priests and Levites 1)

Monday of Week 21: Mal 2:2b–7 (sins of priests and Levites 2)

Tuesday of Week 21: Mal 2:11–17 (sins of the people)

Wednesday of Week 21: Mal 3:5–12, 20b–22 (judgment)

Thursday of Week 21: Hos 1:1–8 (marriage and children)

Friday of Week 21: Hos 2:1–15 (Israel's punishment
    and restoration 1)

Saturday of Week 21: Hos 2:17a, 19–20, 23–25 (Israel's punish-
    ment and restoration 2)

Twenty-second Sunday in Ordinary Time: Hos 3:1–5
    (extra 1–3, love)

Monday of Week 22: Hos 4:1–12 (Israel's crimes, guilt of priests)

Tuesday of Week 22: Hos 4:13–19 (priestly guilt)

Wednesday of Week 22: Hos 5:1–15 (leaders' guilt)

Thursday of Week 22: Hos 6:7—7:7 (violated covenant)

Friday of Week 22: Hos 7:8–12 (foreign alliances)

Saturday of Week 22: Hos 7:13–16 (Israel strayed 1)

Twenty-third Sunday in Ordinary Time: Hos 8:1–3, 8–10, 14
    (Israel strayed 2)

Monday of Week 23: Hos 9:1–6 (exile)

Tuesday of Week 23: Hos 9:7–14 (prophet)

Wednesday of Week 23: Hos 9:15–17; 10:4–6, 9–10
    (Gilgal, idolatry)

Thursday of Week 23: Hos 10:11, 13–15; 11:5–8a, 10–11
(seek the LORD)

Friday of Week 23: Hos 12:1–15 (Israel's infidelity)

Saturday of Week 23: Hos 13:1–8 (furrows of the field)

Twenty-fourth Sunday in Ordinary Time: Hos 13:9—14:1
(Israel destroyed)

Monday of Week 24: Lam 1:1–11 (Jerusalem abandoned 1)

Tuesday of Week 24: Lam 1:12–22 (Jerusalem abandoned 2)

Wednesday of Week 24: Lam 2:1, 3–9, 15–17, 20–22
(the LORD's wrath)

Thursday of Week 24: Lam 3:1–16, 27–30 (suffering)

Friday of Week 24: Lam 3:31–45 (rejection 1)

Saturday of Week 24: Lam3:46–66 (rejection 2)

Twenty-fifth Sunday in Ordinary Time: Lam 4:1–8 (miseries 1)

Monday of Week 25: Lam 4:9–16 (miseries 2)

Tuesday of Week 25: Lam 4:17–22 (miseries 3)

Wednesday of Week 25: Lam 5:1–10 (lament 1)

Thursday of Week 25: Lam 5:11–22 (lament 2)

Friday of Week 25: Bar 1:1–14 (Babylon)

Saturday of Week 25: Bar 2:1–10 (the LORD's justice)

Twenty-sixth Sunday in Ordinary Time: Bar 2:11–26
(deliverance prayer)

Monday of Week 26: Bar 2:27–35 (God's promises 1)

Tuesday of Week 26: Bar 3:1–8 (God's promises 2)

Wednesday of Week 26: Bar 3:16–31 (lack of prudence)

Thursday of Week 26: Bar 4:13–26 (Jerusalem wails)

Friday of Week 26: Bar 4:30–37 (Jerusalem consoled)

Saturday of Week 26: Bar 6:1–14 (Jeremiah's letter 1)

Twenty-seventh Sunday in Ordinary Time: Bar 6:15–28 (Jeremiah's letter 2)

Monday of Week 27: Bar 6:29–39 (Jeremiah's letter 3)

Tuesday of Week 27: Bar 6:40–50 (Jeremiah's letter 4)

Wednesday of Week 27: Bar 6:51–64 (Jeremiah's letter 5)

Thursday of Week 27: Bar 6:65–72 (Jeremiah's letter 6)

Friday of Week 27: 1 Chr 1:1–27 (from Adam to Abraham)

Saturday of Week 27: 1 Chr 1:28–54 (from Abraham to Jacob)

Twenty-eighth Sunday in Ordinary Time: 1 Chr 2:1–55 (Jacob's—Israel's—sons)

Monday of Week 28: 1 Chr 3:1–9 (sons of David)

Tuesday of Week 28: 1 Chr 3:10–24 (sons of Solomon)

Wednesday of Week 28: 1 Chr 4:1–20 (descendants of Judah)

Thursday of Week 28: 1 Chr 4:21–43 (descendants of Shelah)

Friday of Week 28: 1 Chr 5:1–17 (sons of Reuben)

Saturday of Week 28: 1 Chr 5:18–41 (warriors)

Twenty-ninth Sunday in Ordinary Time: 1 Chr 6:1–34 (sons of Levi)

Monday of Week 29: 1 Chr 6:35–66 (descendants of Aaron)

Tuesday of Week 29: 1 Chr 7:1–19 (sons of Issachar)

Wednesday of Week 29: 1 Chr 7:20–40 (sons of Ephraim)

Thursday of Week 29: 1 Chr 8:1–28 (descendants of Benjamin)

Friday of Week 29: 1 Chr 8:29–40 (descendants of Jeiel)

Saturday of Week 29: 1 Chr 9:1–16 (Jerusalem 1)

Thirtieth Sunday in Ordinary Time: 1 Chr 9:17–34 (Jerusalem 2)

Monday of Week 30: 1 Chr 9:35–44 (Saul 1)

Tuesday of Week 30: 1 Chr 10:1–14 (Saul 2)

Wednesday of Week 30: 1 Chr 11:1–21 (David 1)

Thursday of Week 30: 1 Chr 11:22–47 (David 2)

Friday of Week 30: 1 Chr 12:1–19 (David 3)

Saturday of Week 30: 1 Chr 12:20–41 (David 4)

Thirtieth-first Sunday in Ordinary Time: 1 Chr 13:1–14 (transfer of ark 1)

Monday of Week 31: 1 Chr 14:1–7 (transfer of ark 2)

Tuesday of Week 31: 1 Chr 14:8–17 (Philistine wars)

Wednesday of Week 31: 1 Chr 15:1–2, 5–14 (transfer of ark 3)

Thursday of Week 31: 1 Chr 15:17–29 (transfer of ark 4)

Friday of Week 31: 1 Chr 16:3–23 (transfer of ark 5)

Saturday of Week 31: 1 Chr 16:23–43 (transfer of ark 6)

Thirty-second Sunday in Ordinary Time: 1 Chr 17:1–15 (Nathan's oracle)

Monday of Week 32: 1 Chr 17:16–27 (David's prayer)

Tuesday of Week 32: 1 Chr 18:1–8, 17 (David's victories)

Wednesday of Week 32: 1 Chr 19:1–19 (Ammonites 1)

Thursday of Week 32: 1 Chr 20:1–8 (Ammonites 2)

Friday of Week 32: 1 Chr 21:1–15a (David's census)

Saturday of Week 32: 1 Chr 21:15b–30 (Ornan's threshing floor)

Thirty-third Sunday in Ordinary Time: 1 Chr 22:1–19 (material for temple)

Monday of Week 33: 1 Chr 23:1–20 (Levites 1)

Tuesday of Week 33: 1 Chr 23:21–32 (Levites 2)

Wednesday of Week 33: 1 Chr 24:1–31 (priests)

Thursday of Week 33: 1 Chr 25:1–8 (singers 1)

Friday of Week 33: 1 Chr 25:9–31 (singers 2)

Saturday of Week 33: 1 Chr 26:1–19 (gatekeepers)

Solemnity of Christ the King (Thirty-fourth Sunday in Ordinary Time): 1 Chr 26:2--32 (treasurers)

Monday of Week 34: 1 Chr 27:1–15 (army commander)

Tuesday of Week 34: 1 Chr 27:16–34 (tribal heads)

Wednesday of Week 34: 1 Chr 28:1–21 (assembly)

Thursday of Week 34: 1 Chr 29:1–9 (temple offerings)

Friday of Week 34: 1 Chr 29:10–22a (David's prayer)

Saturday of Week 34: 1 Chr 29:22b–30 (Solomon anointed king, David's death)

Ordinary Time Alternative 3

Monday of Week 1: 2 Chr 1:1–12 (Solomon)

Tuesday of Week 1: 2 Chr 1:13–18 (Solomon's wealth)

Wednesday of Week 1: 2 Chr 2:1–9 (temple building 1)

Thursday of Week 1: 2 Chr 2:10–17 (temple building 2)

Friday of Week 1: 2 Chr 3:1–9 (temple building 3)

Saturday of Week 1: 2 Chr 3:10–17 (temple building 4)

Second Sunday in Ordinary Time: 2 Chr 4:1–10 (bronze altar)

Monday of Week 2: 2 Chr 4:11–22 (temple articles)

Tuesday of Week 2: 2 Chr 5:1–5, 11–12 (temple dedication 1)

Wednesday of Week 2: 2 Chr 6:3–11 (Solomon's speech)

Thursday of Week 2: 2 Chr 6:12–21 (Solomon's prayer 1)

Friday of Week 2: 2 Chr 6:22–33 (Solomon's prayer 2)

Saturday of Week 2: 2 Chr 6:34–42 (Solomon's prayer 3)

Third Sunday in Ordinary Time: 2 Chr 7:1–7 (temple dedication 2)

Monday of Week 3: 2 Chr 7:8–16 (eighth day of dedication 1)

Tuesday of Week 3: 2 Chr 7:17–22 (eighth day of dedication 2)

Wednesday of Week 3: 2 Chr 8:1–10 (Solomon's works)

Thursday of Week 3: 2 Chr 8:11–18 (Solomon's piety)

Friday of Week 3: 2 Chr 9:1–14 (queen of Sheba)

Saturday of Week 3: 2 Chr 9:15–31 (things)

Fourth Sunday in Ordinary Time: 2 Chr 10:1–11 (kingdom divided 1)

Monday of Week 4: 2 Chr 10:12–19 (kingdom divided 2)

Tuesday of Week 4: 2 Chr 11:1–12 (Rehoboam 1)

Wednesday of Week 4: 2 Chr 11:13–23 (Rehoboam 2)

Thursday of Week 4: 2 Chr 12:1–8 (Rehoboam 3)

Friday of Week 4: 2 Chr 12:9–16 (Rehoboam 4)

Saturday of Week 4: 2 Chr 13:1–12 (Abijah 1)

Fifth Sunday in Ordinary Time: 2 Chr 13:13–23 (Abijah 2)

Monday of Week 5: 2 Chr 14:1–6 (Asa 1)

Tuesday of Week 5: 2 Chr 14:7–14 (Asa 2)

Wednesday of Week 5: 2 Chr 15:1-11 (Asa 3)

Thursday of Week 5: 2 Chr 15:12–19 (Asa 4)

Friday of Week 5: 2 Chr 16:1–6 (Asa 5)

Saturday of Week 5: 2 Chr 16:7–14 (Asa 6)

Sixth Sunday in Ordinary Time: 2 Chr 17:1–9 (Jehoshaphat 1)

Monday of Week 6: 2 Chr 17:10–19 (Jehoshaphat 2)

Tuesday of Week 6: 2 Chr 18:1–16 (Jehoshaphat 3)

Wednesday of Week 6: 2 Chr 18:17–27 (Jehoshaphat 4)

Thursday of Week 6: 2 Chr 18:28–34 (Jehoshaphat 5)

Friday of Week 6: 2 Chr 19:1–11 (Jehoshaphat 6)

Saturday of Week 6: 2 Chr 20:1–12 (Jehoshaphat 7)

Seventh Sunday in Ordinary Time: 2 Chr 20:13–20
    (Jehoshaphat 8)

Monday of Week 7: 2 Chr 20:21–30 (Jehoshaphat 9)

Tuesday of Week 7: 2 Chr 20:31–37 (Jehoshaphat 10)

Wednesday of Week 7: 2 Chr 21:1–11 (Jehoram 1)

Thursday of Week 7: 2 Chr 21:12–20 (Jehoram 2)

Friday of Week 7: 2 Chr 22:1–9 (Ahaziah 1)

Saturday of Week 7: 2 Chr 22:10–12 (Ahaziah 2)

Eighth Sunday in Ordinary Time: 2 Chr 23:1–11 (Athaliah 1)

Monday of Week 8: 2 Chr 23:12–21 (Athaliah 2)

Tuesday of Week 8: 2 Chr 24:1–7 (Joash 1)

Wednesday of Week 8: 2 Chr 24:8–16, 26–27 (Joash 2)

Thursday of Week 8: 2 Chr 25:1–13 (Amaziah 1)

Friday of Week 8: 2 Chr 25:14–28 (Amaziah 2)

Saturday of Week 8: 2 Chr 26:1–11 (Uzziah 1)

Ninth Sunday in Ordinary Time: 2 Chr 26:12–23 (Uzziah 2)

Monday of Week 9: 2 Chr 27:1–9 (Jotham)

Tuesday of Week 9: 2 Chr 28:1–15 (Ahaz 1)

Wednesday of Week 9: 2 Chr 28:16–27 (Ahaz 2)

Thursday of Week 9: 2 Chr 29:1–11 (Hezekiah 1)

Friday of Week 9: 2 Chr 29:12–30 (Hezekiah 2)

Saturday of Week 9: 2 Chr 29:31–35 (Hezekiah 3)

Tenth Sunday in Ordinary Time: 2 Chr 30:1–13 (Hezekiah 4)

Monday of Week 10: 2 Chr 30:14–27 (Hezekiah 5)

Tuesday of Week 10: 2 Chr 31:1–10 (Hezekiah 6)

Wednesday of Week 10: 2 Chr 31:11–21 (Hezekiah 7)

Thursday of Week 10: 2 Chr 32:1–12 (Sennacherib 1)

Friday of Week 10: 2 Chr 32:10, 13–20 (Sennacherib 2)

Saturday of Week 10: 2 Chr 32:21–26 Hezekiah 8)

Eleventh Sunday in Ordinary Time: 2 Chr 32:27–33 (Hezekiah 9)

Monday of Week 11: 2 Chr 33:1–10 (Manasseh 1)

Tuesday of Week 11: 2 Chr 33:11–20 (Manasseh 2)

Wednesday of Week 11: 2 Chr 33:21–24 (Amon)

Thursday of Week 11: 2 Chr 34:1–7 (Josiah 1)

Friday of Week 11: 2 Chr 34:8–13 (Josiah 2)

Saturday of Week 11: 2 Chr 34:14–25 (Josiah 3)

Twelfth Sunday in Ordinary Time: 2 Chr 34:26–33 (Josiah 4)

Monday of Week 12: 2 Chr 35:1–9 (Josiah 5)

Tuesday of Week 12: 2 Chr 35:10–19 (Josiah 6)

Wednesday of Week 12: 2 Chr 35:20–26 (Josiah 7)

Thursday of Week 12: 2 Chr 36:1–8 (Jehoahaz, Jehoiakim)

Friday of Week 12: 2 Chr 36:9–13, 17–18 (Jehoiachin)

Saturday of Week 12: Ezra 1:7–11 (Cyrus, census 1)

Thirteenth Sunday in Ordinary Time: Ezra 2:1–35 (census 2)

Monday of Week 13: Ezra 2:36–58 (census 3)

Tuesday of Week 13: Ezra 2:59–70 (census 4)

Wednesday of Week 13: Ezra 3:1–6 (rebuilt altar)

Thursday of Week 13: Ezra 3:7–13; 4:1–5 (rebuilt temple 1)

Friday of Week 13: Ezra 4:6–24 (rebuilt temple 2)

Saturday of Week 13: Ezra 5:1–17 (Haggai and Zechariah)

Fourteenth Sunday in Ordinary Time: Ezra 6:1–6
(Darius' decree 1)

Monday of Week 14: Ezra 6:9–12a, 13, 21–22 (Darius' decree 2)

Tuesday of Week 14: Ezra 7:1–28 (Ezra)

Wednesday of Week 14: Ezra 8:1–20 (returnees 1)

Thursday of Week 14: Ezra 8:21–36 (returnees 2)

Friday of Week 14: Ezra 9:1–4, 10–15 (mixed marriages 1)

Saturday of Week 14: Ezra 10:1–8 (mixed marriages 2)

Fifteenth Sunday in Ordinary Time: Ezra 10:9–15
(mixed marriages 3)

Monday of Week 15: Ezra 10:16–44 (mixed marriages 4)

Tuesday of Week 15: Neh 1:1–11 (Nehemiah 1)

Wednesday of Week 15: Neh 2:9–20 (Nehemiah 2)

Thursday of Week 15: Neh 3:1–21 (rebuilding Jerusalem's walls 1)

Friday of Week 15: Neh 3:22–32 (rebuilding Jerusalem's walls 2)

Saturday of Week 15: Neh 3:33—4:17 (rebuilding Jerusalem's walls 3)

Sixteenth Sunday in Ordinary Time: Neh 5:1–13 (food)

Monday of Week 16: Neh 5:14–19 (governor)

Tuesday of Week 16: Neh 6:1–14 (plots against Nehemiah)

Wednesday of Week 16: Neh 6:15–19; 7:1–18 (rebuilt wall, census 1)

Thursday of Week 16: Neh 7:19–60 (census 2)

Friday of Week 16: Neh 7:61–72 (census 3)

Saturday of Week 16: Neh 8:13–18 (feast of Booths)

Seventeenth Sunday in Ordinary Time: Neh 9:1–15 (confession 1)

Monday of Week 17: Neh 9:16–25 (confession 2)

Tuesday of Week 17: Neh 9:26–37 (confession 3)

Wednesday of Week 17: Neh 10:1–28 (agreement 1)

Thursday of Week 17: Neh 10:29–31 (agreement 2)

Friday of Week 17: Neh 10:32–40 (agreement 3)

Saturday of Week 17: Neh 11:1–14 (Jerusalem reopened 1)

Eighteenth Sunday in Ordinary Time: Neh 11:15–36 (Jerusalem reopened 2)

Monday of Week 18: Neh 12:1–11 (priests and Levites 1)

Tuesday of Week 18: Neh 12:12–26 (priests and Levites 2)

Wednesday of Week 18: Neh 12:27–43 (city wall dedicated)

Thursday of Week 18: Neh 12:44–47 (offerings)

Friday of Week 18: Neh 13:1–14 (temple reform)

Saturday of Week 18: Neh 13:15–22 (Sabbath)

Nineteenth Sunday in Ordinary Time: Neh 13:23–31 (mixed marriages)

Monday of Week 19: Tob 1:1–2, 4–8 (Tobit 1)

Tuesday of Week 19: Tob 1:9–22 (Tobit 2)

Wednesday of Week 19: Tob 3:11b–15, 17bc (Sarah's prayer)

Thursday of Week 19: Tob 4:1–11 (Tobit instructs Tobiah 1)

Friday of Week 19: Tob 4:12–21 (Tobit instructs Tobiah 2)

Saturday of Week 19: Tob 5:1–12 (Raphael 1)

Twentieth Sunday in Ordinary Time: Tob 5:13–22 (Raphael 2)

Monday of Week 20: Tob 6:1–9 (journey)

Tuesday of Week 20: Tob 6:12–15 (Sarah 1)

Wednesday of Week 20: Tob 6:16–18 (Sarah 2)

Thursday of Week 20: Tob 7:1c–5 (Raguel)

Friday of Week 20: Tob 8:1–3, 9c–21 (demon expulsion)

Saturday of Week 20: Tob 9:1–6 (money recovered)

Twenty-first Sunday in Ordinary Time: Tob 10:1–7d (Tobiah's parents' anxiety)

Monday of Week 21: Tob 10:7e–14 (Tobiah and Sarah head home)

Tuesday of Week 21: Tob 11:1–4, 18; 12:2–4 (homeward bound)

Wednesday of Week 21: Tob 12: 16–19, 21–22 (Raphael 3)

Thursday of Week 21: Tob 13:10–18 (Tobit's prayer)

Friday of Week 21 Tob 14:1–8 (Tobit's death 1)

Saturday of Week 21: Tob 14:9–15 (Tobit's death 2)

Twenty-second Sunday in Ordinary Time: 1 Macc 1:1–9
    (from Alexander to Antiochus)

Monday of Week 22: 1 Macc 1:16–28 (Antiochus in Judah)

Tuesday of Week 22: 1 Macc 1:29–40 (Mysian commander)

Wednesday of Week 22: 1 Macc 1:44–53, 58–61
    (worship banned)

Thursday of Week 22: 1 Macc 2:1–14, 30–38 (Mattathias 1)

Friday of Week 22: 1 Macc 2:39–48, 53–56, 65–70 (Mattathias 2)

Saturday of Week 22: 1 Macc 3:1–26 (Judas Maccabeus)

Twenty-third Sunday in Ordinary Time: 1 Macc 3:27–37
    (Antiochus' response)

Monday of Week 23: 1 Macc 3:38–59 (victories)

Tuesday of Week 23: 1 Macc 4:1–22 (Gorgias)

Wednesday of Week 23: 1 Macc 4:23–35 (plunder)

Thursday of Week 23: 1 Macc 4:37–51, 60–61 (temple purified)

Friday of Week 23: 1 Macc 5:1–8 (sons of Esau)

Saturday of Week 23: 1 Macc 5:9–32 (Galilean Jews 1)

Twenty-fourth Sunday in Ordinary Time: 1 Macc 5:33–68
    (Galilean Jews 2)

Monday of Week 24: 1 Macc 6:14–27 (Philip succeeds Antiochus)

Tuesday of Week 24: 1 Macc 6:28–46 (campaign against Judas 1)

Wednesday of Week 24: 1 Macc 6:47–63 (campaign against Judas 2)

Thursday of Week 24: 1 Macc 7:1–20 (Demetrius)

Friday of Week 24: 1 Macc 7:21–25 (Alcimus 1)

Saturday of Week 24: 1 Macc 7:26–50 (Nicanor)

Twenty-fifth Sunday in Ordinary Time: 1 Macc 8:1–32 (treaty)

Monday of Week 25: 1 Macc 9:1–10 (Judah invaded)

Tuesday of Week 25: 1 Macc 9:11–22 (death of Judas)

Wednesday of Week 25: 1 Macc 9:23–53 (Jonathan 1)

Thursday of Week 25: 1 Macc 9:54–73 (Alcimus 2, Jonathan 2)

Friday of Week 25: 1 Macc 10:1–20 (revolt of Alexander)

Saturday of Week 25: 1 Macc 10:21–35 (Jonathan and Demetrius 1)

Twenty-sixth Sunday in Ordinary Time: 1 Macc 10:36–50 (Jonathan and Demetrius 2)

Monday of Week 26: 1 Macc 10:51–66 (Ptolemy and Alexander)

Tuesday of Week 26: 1 Macc 10:67–89 (Apollonius)

Wednesday of Week 26: 1 Macc 11:1–13 (Demetrius and Ptolemy)

Thursday of Week 26: 1 Macc 11:14–37 (death of Alexander and Ptolemy)

Friday of Week 26: 1 Macc 11:38–53 (Trypho)

Saturday of Week 26: 1 Macc 11:54–74 (alliance with Trypho)

Twenty-seventh Sunday in Ordinary Time: 1 Macc 12:1–18 (alliance with Rome and Sparta 1)

Monday of Week 27: 1 Macc 12:19–38 (alliance with Rome and Sparta 2)

Tuesday of Week 27: 1 Macc 12:39–53 (Jonathan captured)

Wednesday of Week 27: 1 Macc 13:1–11 (Simon)

Thursday of Week 27: 1 Macc 13:12–24 (deceit of Trypho)

Friday of Week 27: 1 Macc 13:25–42 (Jonathan's death)

Saturday of Week 27: 1 Macc 13:43–51(Simon's deeds 1)

Twenty-eighth Sunday in Ordinary Time: 1 Macc 14:1–3 (Demetrius captured)

Monday of Week 28: 1 Macc 14:4–15 (Simon's deeds 2)

Tuesday of Week 28: 1 Macc 14:16–24 (alliance with Rome and Sparta 3)

Wednesday of Week 28: 1 Macc 14:25–40 (alliance with Rome and Sparta 4)

Thursday of Week 28: 1 Macc 14:41–49 (Simon as leader)

Friday of Week 28: 1 Macc 15:1–14 (Antiochus' letter to Simon)

Saturday of Week 28: 1 Macc 15:15–24 (Roman alliance)

Twenty-ninth Sunday in Ordinary Time: 1 Macc 15:25–41 (Antiochus' hostility)

Monday of Week 29: 1 Macc 16:1–10 (John)

Tuesday of Week 29: 1 Macc 16:11–24 (murder of Simon)

Wednesday of Week 29: 2 Macc 1:1–10 (letter: Jerusalem to Egypt 1)

Thursday of Week 29: 2 Macc 1:11–23 (letter: Jerusalem to Egypt 2)

Friday of Week 29: 2 Macc 1:24–36 (prayer)

Saturday of Week 29: 2 Macc 2:1–8 (background 1)

Thirtieth Sunday in Ordinary Time: 2 Macc 2:9–18a, 32—3:14a (background 2, Heliodorus 1)

Monday of Week 30: 2 Macc 3:14b–24 (Jewish anguish)

Tuesday of Week 30: 2 Macc 3:35–40 (Heliodorus 2)

Wednesday of Week 30: 2 Macc 4:1–17 (Onias)

Thursday of Week 30: 2 Macc 4:18–29 (Jason)

Friday of Week 30: 2 Macc 4:30–38 (Onias murdered)

Saturday of Week 30: 2 Macc 4:39–50 (Lysimachus)

Thirtieth-first Sunday in Ordinary Time: 2 Macc 5:1–20 (Jason's death)

Monday of Week 31: 2 Macc 5:21–27 (Antiochus)

Tuesday of Week 31: 2 Macc 6:1–17 (temple desecrated)

Wednesday of Week 31: 2 Macc 7:3–8, 15–19, 32–42 (mother and sons)

Thursday of Week 31: 2 Macc 8:1–11 (Judas Maccabeus 1)

Friday of Week 31: 2 Macc 8:12–29 (Judas Maccabeus 2)

Saturday of Week 31: 2 Macc 8:30–36 (Judas Maccabeus 3)

Thirty-second Sunday in Ordinary Time: 2 Macc 9:1–18 (Antiochus' death 1)

Monday of Week 32: 2 Macc 9:19–29 (Antiochus' death 2)

Tuesday of Week 32: 2 Macc 10:1–8 (purification of temple)

Wednesday of Week 32: 2 Macc 10:9–23 (Ptolemy's death)

Thursday of Week 32: 2 Macc 10:24–38 (Timothy defeated)

Friday of Week 32: 2 Macc 11:1–15 (Lysias defeated)

Saturday of Week 32: 2 Macc 11:16–38 (letter: Lysias to Jews)

Thirty-third Sunday in Ordinary Time: 2 Macc 12:1–9 (renewed persecution)

Monday of Week 33: 2 Macc 12:10–16 (Judas' deeds 1)

Tuesday of Week 33: 2 Macc 12:17–25 (Judas' deeds 2)

Wednesday of Week 33: 2 Macc 12:26–37 (Judas' deeds 3)

Thursday of Week 33: 2 Macc 12:38–42 (Judas' deeds 4)

Friday of Week 33: 2 Macc 13:1–8 (Menelaus)

Saturday of Week 33: 2 Macc 13:9–26 (Modein)

Solemnity of Christ the King (Thirty-fourth Sunday in Ordinary Time): 2 Macc 14:1–11 (Alcimus)

Monday of Week 34: 2 Macc 14:12–25 (Nicanor 1)

Tuesday of Week 34: 2 Macc 14:26–36 (Nicanor 2)

Wednesday of Week 34: 2 Macc 14:37–46 (Razis)

Thursday of Week 34: 2 Macc 15:1–16 (Nicanor 3)

Friday of Week 34: 2 Macc 15:17–36 (Nicanor 4)

Saturday of Week 34: 2 Macc 15:37–39 (Nicanor 5)

Ordinary Time Alternative 4

Monday of Week 1: Gen 4:16–24, 26 (Cain, Seth)

Tuesday of Week 1: Gen 5:1–7, 9–32 (from Adam to Noah)

Wednesday of Week 1: Gen 6:1–4 (the Nephilim)

Thursday of Week 1: Gen 6:9–22 (Noah: descendants, ark)

Friday of Week 1: Gen 7:6–9, 11–23 (Noah: flood)

Saturday of Week 1: Gen 8:1–5, 14–19; 9:16–17 (Noah: flood ends)

Second Sunday in Ordinary Time: Gen 9:18–29 (Noah and sons)

Monday of Week 2: Gen 10:1–32 (Noah's descendants)

Tuesday of Week 2: Gen 11:10–26 (from Shem to Abram)

Wednesday of Week 2: Gen 11:27–32 (Terah)

Thursday of Week 2: Gen 12:10—13:1, 3–4 (Abram and Sarai in Egypt)

Friday of Week 2: Gen 14:1–17, 21–24 (four kings)

Saturday of Week 2: Gen 15:13–16, 19 (the LORD predicts Egyptian slavery to Abram)

Third Sunday in Ordinary Time: Gen 16:13–14 (the LORD to Hagar)

Monday of Week 3: Gen 17:11–14, 23–27 (circumcision)

Tuesday of Week 3: Gen 19:1–14 (Sodom and Gomorrah)

Wednesday of Week 3: Gen 19:30–38 (Lot)

Thursday of Week 3: Gen 20:1–18 (Abraham, Sarah, Abimelech)

Friday of Week 3: Gen 21:22–34 (pact with Abimelech)

Saturday of Week 3: Gen 22:20–24; 23:5–18, 20 (Nahor's descendants; purchase of cave)

Fourth Sunday in Ordinary Time: Gen 24:9–47, 52–57; 25:1–11 (wife for Isaac; Abraham, Keturah, sons, death)

Monday of Week 4: Gen 25:12–18 (Ishmael's descendants)

Tuesday of Week 4: Gen 25:19–34 (Isaac, Esau, Jacob)

Wednesday of Week 4: Gen 26:1–35 (Isaac, Abimelech)

Thursday of Week 4: Gen 27:6–14, 30–45 (deception of Isaac)

Friday of Week 4: Gen 27:46—28:9 (wife for Jacob)

Saturday of Week 4: Gen 29:1–14a (Jacob and Laban 1)

Fifth Sunday in Ordinary Time: Gen 29:14b–35 (Jacob marries Leah and Rachel)

Monday of Week 5: Gen 30:1–13 (Rachel, Jacob, and Laban 2)

Tuesday of Week 5: Gen 30:14–24 (Rachel, Jacob, and Laban 3)

Wednesday of Week 5: Gen 30:25–36 (Rachel, Jacob, and Laban 4)

Thursday of Week 5: Gen 30:37–43 (Rachel, Jacob, and Laban 5)

Friday of Week 5: Gen 31:1–13 (Jacob leaves Laban 1)

Saturday of Week 5: Gen 31:14–21 (Jacob leaves Laban 2)

Sixth Sunday in Ordinary Time: Gen 31:22–35 (Jacob leaves Laban 3)

Monday of Week 6: Gen 31:36–42 (Jacob leaves Laban 4)

Tuesday of Week 6: Gen 31:43—32:3 (Jacob and Laban 6)

Wednesday of Week 6: Gen 32:4–13 (Jacob and Esau 1)

Thursday of Week 6: Gen 32:14–21 (Jacob and Esau 2)

Friday of Week 6: Gen 33:1–20 (Jacob and Esau 3)

Saturday of Week 6: Gen 34:1–12 (rape of Dinah 1)

Seventh Sunday in Ordinary Time: Gen 34:13–23 (rape of Dinah 2)

Monday of Week 7: Gen 34:24–31; 35:5 (rape of Dinah 3)

Tuesday of Week 7: Gen 35:8–15 (death of Deborah)

Wednesday of Week 7: Gen 35:16–29 (Jacob, Rachel, sons)

Thursday of Week 7: Gen 36:1–19 (Esau, wives, sons 1)

Friday of Week 7: Gen 36:20–43 (Esau, wives, sons 2)

Saturday of Week 7: Gen 37:1–2, 5–11 (Joseph 1)

Eighth Sunday in Ordinary Time: Gen 37:13–17a, 29–36 (Joseph 2)

Monday of Week 8: Gen 38:1–11 (Judah and Tamar 1)

Tuesday of Week 8: Gen 38:12–30 (Judah and Tamar 2)

Wednesday of Week 8: Gen 39:1–10 (Joseph 3)

Thursday of Week 8: Gen 39:11–23 (Joseph 4)

Friday of Week 8: Gen 40:1–15 (Joseph 5)

Saturday of Week 8: Gen 40:16–22 (Joseph 6)

Ninth Sunday in Ordinary Time: Gen 41:1–24 (Joseph 7)

Monday of Week 9: Gen 41:25–46a (Joseph 8)

Tuesday of Week 9: Gen 41:46b–54 (Joseph 9)

Wednesday of Week 9: Gen 42:1–4, 7c–16, 24b–25 (Joseph 10)

Thursday of Week 9: Gen 42:26–38 (Joseph 11)

Friday of Week 9: Gen 43:1–10 (Joseph 12)

Saturday of Week 9: Gen 43:11–23 (Joseph 13)

Tenth Sunday in Ordinary Time: Gen 43:24–34 (Joseph 14)

Monday of Week 10: Gen 44:1–17, 22, 30–34 (Joseph 15)

Tuesday of Week 10: Gen 45:6–15 (Joseph 16)

Wednesday of Week 10: Gen 45:16–28 (Joseph 17)

Thursday of Week 10: Gen 46:8–27 (Joseph 18)

Friday of Week 10: Gen 46:31—47:12 (Joseph 19)

Saturday of Week 10: Gen 47:13–26 (Joseph 20)

Eleventh Sunday in Ordinary Time: Gen 47:27–31 (Joseph 21)

Monday of Week 11: Gen 48:1–11 (Joseph 22)

Tuesday of Week 11: Gen 48:12–22 (Joseph 23)

Wednesday of Week 11: Gen 49:1–8 (Joseph 24)

Thursday of Week 11: Gen 49:11–27 (Joseph 25)

Friday of Week 11: Gen 49:28, 33—50:9 (Joseph 26)

Saturday of Week 11: Gen 50:11–14, 26b (Joseph 27)

Twelfth Sunday in Ordinary Time: Exod 1:1–6, 15–20
    (Jacob's descendants in Egypt)

Monday of Week 12: Exod 2:15c–25 (Moses in Midian)

Tuesday of Week 12: Exod 3:21–22; 4:1–9 (Moses; mission)

Wednesday of Week 12: Exod 4:10–17 (Moses' assistant: Aaron)

Thursday of Week 12: Exod 4:18–31 (Moses and Aaron
    go to Egypt)

Friday of Week 12: Exod 5:1–23 (Moses, Aaron, Pharoah 1)

Saturday of Week 12: Exod 6:1–13 (Moses, Aaron, Pharaoh 2)

Thirteenth Sunday in Ordinary Time: Exod 6:14–27
    (genealogy of Moses and Aaron)

Monday of Week 13: Exod 6:28–30; 7:1–13 (Moses, Aaron,
    Pharaoh 3)

Tuesday of Week 13: Exod 7:14–24 (plague 1: water to blood)

Wednesday of Week 13: Exod 7:25—8:ll (plague 2: frogs)

Thursday of Week 13: Exod 8:12–15 (plague 3: gnats)

Friday of Week 13: Exod 8:16–28 (plague 4: flies)

Saturday of Week 13: Exod 9:1–7 (plague 5: pestilence)

Fourteenth Sunday in Ordinary Time: Exod 9:8–12
(plague 6: boils)

Monday of Week 14: Exod 9:13–35 (plague 7: hail)

Tuesday of Week 14: Exod 10:1–11 (plague 8: locusts 1)

Wednesday of Week 14: 10:12–20 (plague 8: locusts 2)

Thursday of Week 14: Exod 10:21–29 (plague 9: darkness)

Friday of Week 14: Exod 11:1–9; 12:27c–30 (plague 10:
death of first-born)

Saturday of Week 14: Exod 12:15–20 (unleavened bread)

Fifteenth Sunday in Ordinary Time: Exod 12:31–36
(departure from Egypt)

Monday of Week 15: Exod 12:43–50 (Passover regulations)

Tuesday of Week 15: Exod 13:1–16 (consecration of first-born)

Wednesday of Week 15: Exod 13:17–22 (toward the Red Sea 1)

Thursday of Week 15: Exod 14:1–4 (toward the Red Sea 2)

Friday of Week 15: Exod 15:18–27 (through the Red Sea to Shur)

Saturday of Week 15: Exod 16:6–8, 16–20 (manna 1)

Sixteenth Sunday in Ordinary Time: Gen 16:21–36 (manna 2)

Monday of Week 16: Exod 17:14–15; 18:1–12
(Amalek, Moses, Jethro)

Tuesday of Week 16: Gen 18:13–27 (Moses appoints judges)

Wednesday of Week 16: Exod 19:12, 21–25 (limits at Sinai)

Thursday of Week 16: Exod 20:18–26 (fear of God)

Friday of Week 16: Exod 21:1–11 (slaves)

Saturday of Week 16: Exod 21:12–25 (personal injury 1)

Seventeenth Sunday in Ordinary Time: Exod 21:26–32 (personal injury 2)

Monday of Week 17: Exod 21:33–37 (personal injury 3)

Tuesday of Week 17: Exod 22:1–5 (property damage)

Wednesday of Week 17: Exod 22:6–19 (trusts, loans, social laws 1)

Thursday of Week 17: Exod 22:27–30 (trusts, loans, social laws 2)

Friday of Week 17: Exod 23:1–9 (trusts, loans, social laws 3)

Saturday of Week 17: Exod 23:10–19 (religious laws 1)

Eighteenth Sunday in Ordinary Time: Exod 23:24–33 (religious laws 2)

Monday of Week 18: Exod 24:1–2, 9–18 (covenant ratification)

Tuesday of Week 18: Exod 25:1–22 (dwelling 1)

Wednesday of Week 18: Exod 25:23–40 (dwelling 2)

Thursday of Week 18: Exod 26:1–14 (dwelling 3)

Friday of Week 18: Exod 26:15–30 (dwelling 4)

Saturday of Week 18: Exod 26:31–37 (dwelling 5)

Nineteenth Sunday in Ordinary Time: Exod 27:1–21 (dwelling 6)

Monday of Week 19: Exod 28:1–30 (dwelling 7)

Tuesday of Week 19: Exod 28:31–43 (dwelling 8)

Wednesday of Week 19: Exod 29:1–9 (priests 1)

Thursday of Week 19: 29:10–28 (priests 2)

Friday of Week 19: Exod 29:29–37 (priest 3)

Saturday of Week 19: Exod 29:38–46 (priests 4)

Twentieth Sunday in Ordinary Time: Exod 30:17–38 (dwelling 9)

Monday of Week 20: Exod 31:1–11 (artisans 1)

Tuesday of Week 20: Exod 31:12–18 (Sabbath)

Wednesday of Week 20: Exod 32:1–6, 25–29, 35 (golden calf)

Thursday of Week 20: Exod 33:1–6 (bad news, good news 1)

Friday of Week 20: Exod 33:12–23 (bad news, good news 2)

Saturday of Week 20: Exod 34:1–3, 10–17 (tablets renewed 1)

Twenty-first Sunday in Ordinary Time: Exod 34:18–27 (tablets renewed 2)

Monday of Week 21: Exod 35:1–3 (tablets renewed 3)

Tuesday of Week 21: Exod 35:4–19 (materials collected, artisans 2)

Wednesday of Week 21: Exod 35:20–35 (contributions, artisans 3)

Thursday of Week 21: Exod 36:1–19 (dwelling built 1)

Friday of Week 21: Exod 36:20–38 (dwelling built 2)

Saturday of Week 21: Exod 37:1–16 (dwelling built 3)

Twenty-second Sunday in Ordinary Time: Exod 37:17–29 (dwelling built 4)

Monday of Week 22: Exod 38:1–8 (dwelling built 5)

Tuesday of Week 22: Exod 38:9–20 (dwelling built 6)

Wednesday of Week 22: Exod 38:21–31 (dwelling built 7)

Thursday of Week 22: Exod 39:1–7 (dwelling built 8)

Friday of Week 22: Exod 39:8–21 (dwelling built 9)

Saturday of Week 22: Exod 39:22–31 (dwelling built 10)

Twenty-third Sunday in Ordinary Time: Exod 39:32–43 (dwelling built 11)

Monday of Week 23: Exod 40:1–15 (dwelling built 12)

Tuesday of Week 23: Exod 40:22–33 (dwelling built 13)

Wednesday of Week 23: Lev 1:1–7 (holocausts)

Thursday of Week 23: Lev 2:1–16 (cereal offerings)

Friday of Week 23: Lev 3:1–17 (peace offerings)

Saturday of Week 23: Lev 4:1–12 (sin offerings for priests)

Twenty-fourth Sunday in Ordinary Time: Lev 4:13–26
(sin offerings for the community)

Monday of Week 24: Lev 4:27–35 (sin offerings for individuals)

Tuesday of Week 24: Lev 5:1–13 (special cases offerings)

Wednesday of Week 24: Lev 5:14–26 (guilt offerings)

Thursday of Week 24: Lev 6:1–11 (daily holocaust, cereal, sin 1)

Friday of Week 24: Lev 6:12–23 (daily holocaust, cereal sin 2)

Saturday of Week 24: Lev 7:1–21 (guilt and peace offerings)

Twenty-fifth Sunday in Ordinary Time: Lev 7:22–38
(blood and fat)

Monday of Week 25: Lev 8:1–21 (ordination: Aaron and sons 1)

Tuesday of Week 25: Lev 8:22–36 (ordination: Aaron and sons 2)

Wednesday of Week 25: Lev 9:1–14 (octave of ordination 1)

Thursday of Week 25: Lev 9:15–24 (octave of ordination 2)

Friday of Week 25: Lev 10:1–11 (Nadab and Abihu)

Saturday of Week 25: Lev 10:12–20 (priestly portion)

Twenty-sixth Sunday in Ordinary Time: Lev 11:1–23
(clean and unclean food 1)

Monday of Week 26: Lev 11:24–47 (clean and unclean food 2)

Tuesday of Week 26: Lev 12:1–8 (childbirth uncleanness)

Wednesday of Week 26: Lev 13:3–23 (leprosy 1)

Thursday of Week 26: Lev 13:26–43 (leprosy 2)

Friday of Week 26: Lev 13:47–59 (leprosy 3)

Saturday of Week 26: Lev 14:1–9 (leprosy 4)

Twenty-seventh Sunday in Ordinary Time: Lev 14:10–20
    (leprosy 5)

Monday of Week 27: Lev 14:21–32 (leprosy 6)

Tuesday of Week 27: Lev 14:33–57 (leprosy 7)

Wednesday of Week 27: Lev 15:1–18 (uncleanness 1)

Thursday of Week 27: Lev 15:19–33 (uncleanness 2)

Friday of Week 27: Lev 16:1–19 (day of atonement 1)

Saturday of Week 27: Lev 16:20–34 (the scapegoat)

Twenty-eighth Sunday in Ordinary Time: Lev 17:1–15 (blood)

Monday of Week 28: Lev 18:1–15 (sex 1)

Tuesday of Week 28: Lev 18:16–30 (sex 2)

Wednesday of Week 28: Lev 19:3–10, 15a, 19–37
    (rules of conduct)

Thursday of Week 28: Lev 20:1–14 (sins and penalties 1)

Friday of Week 28: Lev 20:15–27 (sins and penalties 2)

Saturday of Week 28: Lev 21:1–12 (priests 1)

Twenty-ninth Sunday in Ordinary Time: Lev 21:13–24 (priests 2)

Monday of Week 29: Lev 22:1–16 (sacrificial banquets)

Tuesday of Week 29: Lev 22:17–32 (unacceptable victims)

Wednesday of Week 29: Lev 23:2–3, 12–14, 17–25 (holy days)

Thursday of Week 29: Lev 23:28–32 (day of atonement 2)

Friday of Week 29: Lev 23:38–44 (days of rest)

Saturday of Week 29: Lev 24:1–9 (sanctuary lamp, showbread)

Thirtieth Sunday in Ordinary Time: Lev 24:10–24 (blasphemy)

Monday of Week 30: Lev 25:2–7, 18–22 (sabbatical year)

Tuesday of Week 30: Lev 25: 23–31 (redemption of property 1)

Wednesday of Week 30: Lev 25:32–43 (redemption of property 2)

Thursday of Week 30: Lev 25:44–55 (redemption of property 3)

Friday of Week 30: Lev 26:1–13 (obedience)

Saturday of Week 30: Lev 26:14–35 (disobedience 1)

Thirtieth-first Sunday in Ordinary Time: Lev 26:36–46
    (disobedience 2)

Monday of Week 31: Lev 27:1–13 (votive offerings 1)

Tuesday of Week 31: Lev 27:14–25 (votive offerings 2)

Wednesday of Week 31: Lev 27:26–34 (offerings not redeemed)

Thursday of Week 31: Num 1:1–27 (census 1)

Friday of Week 31: Num 1:28–46 (census 2)

Saturday of Week 31: Num 1:47–54 (census 3)

Thirty-second Sunday in Ordinary Time: Num 2:1–17
    (camp arrangement 1)

Monday of Week 32: Num 2:18–34 (camp arrangement 2)

Tuesday of Week 32: Num 3:1–4, 10–13 (Aaron's sons)

Wednesday of Week 32: Num 3:14–20 (Levites' census 1)

Thursday of Week 32: Num 3:21–51 (duties of Levites)

Friday of Week 32: Num 4:1–20 (Kohathites)

Saturday of Week 32: Num 4:21–33 (Gershanites)

Thirty-third Sunday in Ordinary Time: Num 4:34–49 (Levites 1)

Monday of Week 33: Num 5:1–10 (camp expulsion 1)

Tuesday of Week 33: Num 5:11–31 (camp expulsion 2)

Wednesday of Week 33: Num 6:1–21 (Nazirites)

Thursday of Week 33: Num 7:1–11 (offerings 1)

Friday of Week 33: Num 7:12–23 (offerings 2)

Saturday of Week 33: Num 7:24–35 (offerings 3)

Solemnity of Christ the King (Thirty-fourth Sunday in Ordinary Time): Num 7:36–47 (offerings 4)

Monday of Week 34: Num 7:48–59 (offerings 5)

Tuesday of Week 34: Num 7:60–77 (offerings 6)

Wednesday of Week 34: Num 7:78–89 (offerings 7)

Thursday of Week 34: Num 8:1–14 (lamps, Levites 2)

Friday of Week 34: Num 8:15–26 (lamps, Levites 3)

Saturday of Week 34: Num 9:1–14 (Passover)

Ordinary Time Alternative 5

Monday of Week 1: Num 9:1–14 (Passover)

Tuesday of Week 1: Num 9:15–23 (fiery cloud over dwelling)

Wednesday of Week 1: Num 10:1–10 (trumpets)

Thursday of Week 1: Num 10:11–36 (from Sinai and Moab)

Friday of Week 1: Num 11:1–4, 18–23, 31–35 (quail)

Saturday of Week 1: Num 12:14–16 (Miriam's leprosy)

Second Sunday in Ordinary Time: Num 13:3–24 (scouts)

Monday of Week 2: Num 14:2–25, 30–33, 36–45
(grumbling, Caleb)

Tuesday of Week 2: Num 15:1–21 (offerings 8)

Wednesday of Week 2: Num 15:22–31 (offerings 9)

Thursday of Week 2: Num 15:32–41 (Sabbath, tassels)

Friday of Week 2: Num 16:1–11, 16–24, 35 (Korah)

Saturday of Week 2: Num 16:12–15, 25–34 (Dathan, Abiram)

Third Sunday in Ordinary Time: Num 17:1–15 (census 4)

Monday of Week 3: Num 17:16–28 (Aaron's staff)

Tuesday of Week 3: Num 18:1–7 (sanctuary)

Wednesday of Week 3: Num 18:8–20 (priests' share of sacrifices)

Thursday of Week 3: Num 18:21–32 (tithes due Levites)

Friday of Week 3: Num 19:1–22 (red heifer ashes)

Saturday of Week 3: Num 20:14–29 (king of Edom)

Fourth Sunday in Ordinary Time: Num 21:1–3, 10–20
(king of Arod, around Moab)

Monday of Week 4: Num 21:21–35 (king of Amorites,
king of Bashan)

Tuesday of Week 4: Num 22:1–22 (Balaam 1)

Wednesday of Week 4: Num 22:23–39 (Balaam 2)

Thursday of Week 4: Num 22:41—23:12 (Balaam 3)

Friday of Week 4: Num 23:13–26 (Balaam 4)

Saturday of Week 4: Num 23:27—24:1, 8–13 (Balaam 5)

Fifth Sunday in Ordinary Time: Num 24:14, 17c–25 (Balaam 6)

Monday of Week 5: Num 25:1–18 (Baal)

Tuesday of Week 5: Num 26:1–25 (second census 1)

Wednesday of Week 5: Num 26:26–56 (second census 2)

Thursday of Week 5: Num 26:57–65 (Levites' census 2)

Friday of Week 5: Num 27:1–11 (heiress daughters)

Saturday of Week 5: Num 27:12–23 (Moses' successor: Joshua)

Sixth Sunday in Ordinary Time: Num 28:1–10 (sacrifices: morning, evening, Sabbath)

Monday of Week 6: Num 28:11–31 (sacrifices: new moon, Passover, Pentecost)

Tuesday of Week 6: Num 29:1–39 (sacrifices: new year's day, atonement)

Wednesday of Week 6: Num 30:1–17 (vows)

Thursday of Week 6: Num 31:1–18 (Midianites 1)

Friday of Week 6: Num 31:19–31 (Midianites 2)

Saturday of Week 6: Num 31:32–54 (Midianites 3)

Seventh Sunday in Ordinary Time: Num 32:1–15 (Gad and Reuben 1)

Monday of Week 7: Num 32:16–42 (Gad and Reuben 2)

Tuesday of Week 7: Num 33:1–15 (journey stages 1)

Wednesday of Week 7: Num 33:16–41 (journey stages 2)

Thursday of Week 7: Num 33:42–56 (journey stages 3)

Friday of Week 7: Num 34:1–15 (boundaries)

Saturday of Week 7: Num 34:16–29 (supervisors)

Eighth Sunday in Ordinary Time: Num 35:1–15 (Levite cities, cities of asylum 1)

Monday of Week 8: Num 35:16–34 (cities of asylum 2)

Tuesday of Week 8: Num 36:1–13 (heiresses' property)

Wednesday of Week 8: Deut 1:1–8, 15–18 (Horeb)

Thursday of Week 8: Deut 1:19–36 (scouts)

Friday of Week 8: Deut 1:37–45 (the LORD's anger)

Saturday of Week 8: Deut 2:1–15 (Red Sea Road)

Ninth Sunday in Ordinary Time: Deut 2:16–37 (Ammonites)

Monday of Week 9: Deut 3:1–11 (Bashan)

Tuesday of Week 9: Deut 3:12–29 (conquered lands)

Wednesday of Week 9: Deut 4:3–4, 10–14 (fidelity)

Thursday of Week 9: Deut 4:15–24 (idolatry 1)

Friday of Week 9: Deut 4:25–31, 41–43 (God's fidelity)

Saturday of Week 9: Deut 4:44—5:4 (covenant)

Tenth Sunday in Ordinary Time: Deut 5:6–11, 16–21 (decalogue)

Monday of Week 10: Deut 5:22–33 (the LORD's words)

Tuesday of Week 10: Deut 6:14–19 (other gods 1)

Wednesday of Week 10: Deut 6:20–25 (other gods 2)

Thursday of Week 10: Deut 7:1–5, 12–26 (destruction of enemies)

Friday of Week 10: Deut 8:1, 4–6, 19–20 (God's love)

Saturday of Week 10: Deut 9:1–6 (success)

Eleventh Sunday in Ordinary Time: Deut 9:7–19 (golden calf 1)

Monday of Week 11: Deut 9:20–29 (golden calf 2)

Tuesday of Week 11: Deut 10:1–7, 10–11 (new tablets)

Wednesday of Week 11: Deut 11:1–6 (love God)

Thursday of Week 11: Deut 11:10–17 (rain)

Friday of Week 11: Deut 11:19–25, 29–31 (teach children)

Saturday of Week 11: Deut 12:1–14 (sanctuary)

Twelfth Sunday in Ordinary Time: Deut 12:15–19 (meals 1)

Monday of Week 12: Deut 12:20–31 (meals 2)

Tuesday of Week 12: Deut 13:1–19 (idolatry 2)

Wednesday of Week 12: Deut 14:1–10 (clean and unclean 1)

Thursday of Week 12: Deut 14:11–29 (clean and unclean 2)

Friday of Week 12: Deut 15:1–11 (debts)

Saturday of Week 12: Deut 15:12–18 (slaves)

Thirteenth Sunday in Ordinary Time: Deut 15:19–23 (firstlings)

Monday of Week 13: Deut 16:1–8 (Passover)

Tuesday of Week 13: Deut 16:9–12 (Weeks)

Wednesday of Week 13: Deut 16:13–17 (Booths)

Thursday of Week 13: Deut 16:18–22 (judges 1)

Friday of Week 13: Deut 17:1–7 (sacrifices)

Saturday of Week 13: Deut 17:8–13 (judges 2)

Fourteenth Sunday in Ordinary Time: Deut 17:14–20 (kings)

Monday of Week 14: Deut 18:1–14, 21–22 (priests)

Tuesday of Week 14: Deut 19:1–10 (cities of refuge 1)

Wednesday of Week 14: Deut 19:11–14 (cities of refuge 2)

Thursday of Week 14: Deut 19:15–21 (cities of refuge 3)

Friday of Week 14: Deut 20:1–9 (courage 1)

Saturday of Week 14: Deut 20:10–18 (courage 2)

Fifteenth Sunday in Ordinary Time: Deut 20:19–20 (trees)

Monday of Week 15: Deut 21:1–9 (murder)

Tuesday of Week 15: Deut 21:10–14 (female captives)

Wednesday of Week 15: Deut 21:15–23 (sons)

Thursday of Week 15: Deut 22:1–12 (lost animals)

Friday of Week 15: Deut 22:13–21 (marriage 1)

Saturday of Week 15: Deut 22:22—23:1 (marriage 2)

Sixteenth Sunday in Ordinary Time: Deut 23:2–9 (membership)

Monday of Week 16: Deut 23:10–15 (camp)

Tuesday of Week 16: Deut 23:16–21 (various precepts 1)

Wednesday of Week 16: Deut 23:22–26 (various precepts 2)

Thursday of Week 16: Deut 24:1–5 (marriage 3)

Friday of Week 16: Deut 24:6–16; 25:1–4 (justice)

Saturday of Week 16: Deut 25:5–10 (levirate marriage)

Seventeenth Sunday in Ordinary Time: Deut 25:11–19 (various precepts 3)

Monday of Week 17: Deut 26:1–3, 11–15 (thanksgiving for the harvest)

Tuesday of Week 17: Deut 27:1–13 (crossing the Jordan)

Wednesday of Week 17: Deut 27:14–26 (curses 1)

Thursday of Week 17: Deut 28:1–6 (blessings 1)

Friday of Week 17: Deut 28:7–14 (blessings 2)

Saturday of Week 17: Deut 28:15–29a (curses 2)

Eighteenth Sunday in Ordinary Time: Deut 28:29b–35 (exile 1)

Monday of Week 18: Deut 29:36–48 (exile 2)

Tuesday of Week 18: Deut 28:49–57 (invasion)

Wednesday of Week 18: Deut 28:58–69 (plagues)

Thursday of Week 18: Deut 29:1–14 (past favors)

Friday of Week 18: Deut 29:15–28 (idolatry 3)

Saturday of Week 18: Deut 30:5–10 (promised land)

Nineteenth Sunday in Ordinary Time: Deut 31:9–15 (law 1)

Monday of Week 19: Deut 31:16–22 (Joshua commissioned)

Tuesday of Week 19: Deut 31:23–30 (law 2)

Wednesday of Week 19: Deut 32:44–52 (law 3)

Thursday of Week 19: Deut 33:1–12 (blessing of tribes 1)

Friday of Week 19: Deut 33:13–29 (blessing of tribes 2)

Saturday of Week 19: Josh 1:1–18 (divine assistance)

Twentieth Sunday in Ordinary Time: Josh 2:1–14 (spies 1)

Monday of Week 20: Josh 2:15–24 (spies 2)

Tuesday of Week 20: Josh 3:1–6 (preparing to cross the Jordan)

Wednesday of Week 20: Josh 4:1–7 (memorial stones 1)

Thursday of Week 20: Josh 4:8–14 (memorial stones 2)

Friday of Week 20: Josh 4:15–24 (crossing the Jordan)

Saturday of Week 20: Josh 5:1–8 (Gilgal)

Twenty-first Sunday in Ordinary Time: Josh 5:13—6:5 (Jericho 1)

Monday of Week 21: Josh 6:6–19 (Jericho 2)

Tuesday of Week 21: Josh 6:20–27 (Jericho 3)

Wednesday of Week 21: Josh 7:1–15 (Ai 1)

Thursday of Week 21: Josh 7:16–26 (Achan)

Friday of Week 21 Josh 8:1–17 (Ai 2)

Saturday of Week 21: Josh 8:18–29 (Ai 3)

Twenty-second Sunday in Ordinary Time: Josh 9:1–15
    (confederacy against Israel 1)

Monday of Week 22: Josh 9:16–27 (Gibeon 1)

Tuesday of Week 22: Josh 10:1–15 (Gibeon 2)

Wednesday of Week 22: Josh 10:16–27 (Amorite kings)

Thursday of Week 22: Josh 10:28–43 (southern Canaan)

Friday of Week 22: Josh 11:1–9 (confederacy against Israel 2)

Saturday of Week 22: Josh 11:10–15 (confederacy against Israel 3)

Twenty-third Sunday in Ordinary Time: Josh 11:16–23
    (conquest)

Monday of Week 23: Josh 12:1–22 (defeated kings)

Tuesday of Week 23: Josh 13:1–14 (division of land 1)

Wednesday of Week 23: Josh 13:15–33 (division of land 2)

Thursday of Week 23: Josh 14:1–8 (division of land 3)

Friday of Week 23: Josh 14:9–15 (division of land 4)

Saturday of Week 23: Josh 15:1–12 (division of land 5)

Twenty-fourth Sunday in Ordinary Time: Josh 15:13–19
    (division of land 6)

Monday of Week 24: Josh 15:20–47 (division of land 7)

Tuesday of Week 24: Josh 15:48–63 (division of land 8)

Wednesday of Week 24: Josh 16:1–10 (division of land 9)

Thursday of Week 24: Josh 17:1–13 (division of land 10)

Friday of Week 24: Josh 17:14–18 (division of land 11)

Saturday of Week 24: Josh 18:1–10 (division of land 12)

Twenty-fifth Sunday in Ordinary Time: Josh 18:11–28 (division of land 13)

Monday of Week 25: Josh 19:1–23 (division of land 14)

Tuesday of Week 25: Josh 19:24–51 (division of land 15)

Wednesday of Week 25: Josh 20:1–9 (asylum cities)

Thursday of Week 25: Josh 21:1–8 (Levitical cities)

Friday of Week 25: Josh 21:9–19 (priestly cities)

Saturday of Week 25: Josh 21:20–26 (Kohathites cities)

Twenty-sixth Sunday in Ordinary Time: Josh 21:27–33 (Gershonites cities)

Monday of Week 26: Josh 21:34–45 (Merarites cities)

Tuesday of Week 26: Josh 22:1–9 (eastern tribes 1)

Wednesday of Week 26: Josh 22:10–12 (eastern tribes 2)

Thursday of Week 26: Josh 22:13–20 (western tribes)

Friday of Week 26: Josh 22:21–34 (Phinehas)

Saturday of Week 26: Josh 23:1–16 (Joshua's farewell 1)

Twenty-seventh Sunday in Ordinary Time: Josh 24:29–33 (Joshua's farewell 2)

Monday of Week 27: Judg 1:1–20 (post-Joshua 1)

Tuesday of Week 27: Judg 1:21–36 (post-Joshua 2)

Wednesday of Week 27: Judg 2:1–10, 20–23 (Israelites' infidelity)

Thursday of Week 27: Judg 3:1–6 (other nations)

Friday of Week 27: Judg 3:7–31 (Othniel, Ehud)

Saturday of Week 27: Judg 4:1–11 (Deborah and Barak 1)

Twenty-eighth Sunday in Ordinary Time: Judg 4:12–24
(Deborah and Barak 2)

Monday of Week 28: Judg 5:1–15 (Deborah's canticle 1)

Tuesday of Week 28: Judg 5:16–31 (Deborah's canticle 2)

Wednesday of Week 28: Judg 6:1–10 (Gideon 1)

Thursday of Week 28: Judg 6:25–32 (Gideon 2)

Friday of Week 28: Judg 6:33–40 (Gideon 3)

Saturday of Week 28: Judg 7:1–12 (Gideon 4)

Twenty-ninth Sunday in Ordinary Time: Judg 7:13–18
(Gideon 5)

Monday of Week 29: Judg 7:19–25 (Gideon 6)

Tuesday of Week 29: Judg 8:1–17 (Gideon 7)

Wednesday of Week 29: Judg 8:18–35 (Gideon 8)

Thursday of Week 29: Judg 9:1–5, 16–21 (Abimelech 1)

Friday of Week 29: Judg 9:22–29 (Abimelech 2)

Saturday of Week 29: Judg 9:30–41 (Abimelech 3)

Thirtieth Sunday in Ordinary Time: Judg 9:42–49 (Abimelech 4)

Monday of Week 30: Judg 9:50–57 (Abimelech 5)

Tuesday of Week 30: Judg 10:1–18 (Tola)

Wednesday of Week 30: Judg 11:1–13 (Jephthah 1)

Thursday of Week 30: Judg 11:14–28 (Jephthah 2)

Friday of Week 30: Judg 12:1–7 (Jephthah 3)

Saturday of Week 30: Judg 12:8–15 (Ibzan, Elon, Abdon)

Thirtieth-first Sunday in Ordinary Time: Judg 13:1, 8–14
(Samson 1)

Monday of Week 31: Judg 13:15–23 (Samson 2)

Tuesday of Week 31: Judg 14:1–10 (Samson 3)

Wednesday of Week 31: Judg 14:11–20 (Samson 4)

Thursday of Week 31: Judg 15:1–8 (Samson 5)

Friday of Week 31: Judg 15:9–20 (Samson 6)

Saturday of Week 31: Judg 16:1–14 (Samson 7)

Thirty-second Sunday in Ordinary Time: Judg 16:15–22 (Samson 8)

Monday of Week 32: Judg 16:23–31 (Samson 9)

Tuesday of Week 32: Judg 17:1–13 (Micah and the Levite)

Wednesday of Week 32: Judg 18:1–15 (Danites 1)

Thursday of Week 32: Judg 18:16–31 (Danites 2)

Friday of Week 32: Judg 19:1–21 (Levite from Ephraim)

Saturday of Week 32: Judg 19:22–30 (outrage at Gibeah)

Thirty-third Sunday in Ordinary Time: Judg 20:1–19 (Israelites assemble)

Monday of Week 33: Judg 20:20–35 (war with Benjamin 1)

Tuesday of Week 33: Judg 20:36–48 (war with Benjamin 2)

Wednesday of Week 33: Judg 21:1–5 (wives for Benjaminites 1)

Thursday of Week 33: Judg 21:6–14 (wives for Benjaminites 2)

Friday of Week 33: Judg 21:15–25 (wives for Benjaminites 3)

Saturday of Week 33: Ruth 1:2, 7–14, 17–21 (Naomi)

Solemnity of Christ the King (Thirty-fourth Sunday in Ordinary Time): Ruth 2:4–7, 12–16 (Boaz 1)

Monday of Week 34: Ruth 2:17–23 (Boaz 2)

Tuesday of Week 34: Ruth 3:1–15 (Ruth 1)

Wednesday of Week 34: Ruth 3:16–18 (Ruth 2)

Thursday of Week 34: Ruth 4:1–4 (Boaz and Ruth 1)

Friday of Week 34: Ruth 4:5–12 (Boaz and Ruth 2)

Saturday of Week 34: Ruth 4:18–22 (David's ancestors)

Ordinary Time Alternative 6

Monday of Week 1: 1 Sam 1:23; 2:11, 18–21 (Samuel)

Tuesday of Week 1: 1 Sam 2:12–17, 22–26 (Eli and sons 1)

Wednesday of Week 1: 1 Sam 2:27–36 (Eli and sons 2)

Thursday of Week 1: 1 Sam 3:11–18, 21 (fate of Eli and sons)

Friday of Week 1: 1 Sam 4:12–22 (death of Eli)

Saturday of Week 1: 1 Sam 5:1–12 (ark 1)

Second Sunday in Ordinary Time: 1 Sam 6:1–16 (ark 2)

Monday of Week 2: 1 Sam 6:17–21 (ark 3)

Tuesday of Week 2: 1 Sam 7:1–17 (ark 4)

Wednesday of Week 2: 1 Sam 8:1–3, 8–9 (request for a king)

Thursday of Week 2: 1 Sam 9:5–13 (Saul 1)

Friday of Week 2: 1 Sam 9:14–16, 20–27 (Saul 2)

Saturday of Week 2: 1 Sam 10:1b–13 (Saul 3)

Third Sunday in Ordinary Time: 1 Sam 10:14–27 (Saul 4)

Monday of Week 3: 1 Sam 11:1–8 (Ammonites 1)

Tuesday of Week 3: 1 Sam 11:9–16 (Ammonites 2)

Wednesday of Week 3: 1 Sam 12:1–12 (Samuel addresses Israel 1)

Thursday of Week 3: 1 Sam 13:13–25 (Samuel addresses Israel 2)

Friday of Week 3: 1 Sam 13:1–14 (Saul 5)

Saturday of Week 3: 1 Sam 13:15–23 (Saul 6)

Fourth Sunday in Ordinary Time: 1 Sam 14:1–15 (Jonathan 1)

Monday of Week 4: 1 Sam 14:16–30 (Jonathan 2)

Tuesday of Week 4: 1 Sam 14:31–44 (Jonathan 3)

Wednesday of Week 4: 1 Sam 14:45–52 (Jonathan 4)

Thursday of Week 4: 1 Sam 15:1–9 (Samuel and Saul 1)

Friday of Week 4: 1 Sam 15:10–15 (Samuel and Saul 2)

Saturday of Week 4: 1 Sam 15:24–35 (Samuel and Saul 3)

Fifth Sunday in Ordinary Time: 1 Sam 16:14–18
 (Saul's melancholy 1)

Monday of Week 5: 1 Sam 16:19–23 (Saul's melancholy 2)

Tuesday of Week 5: 1 Sam 17:1–11 (Goliath 1)

Wednesday of Week 5: 1 Sam 17:12–31, 34–36, 38–39 (Goliath 2)

Thursday of Week 5: 1 Sam 17:52–58 (Goliath 3)

Friday of Week 5: 1 Sam 18:1–5, 10–19 (David and Jonathan 1)

Saturday of Week 5: 1 Sam 18:20–30 (Michal)

Sixth Sunday in Ordinary Time: 1 Sam 19:8–17
 (David vs. Philistine)

Monday of Week 6: 1 Sam 19:18–21 (David, Samuel, Saul 1)

Tuesday of Week 6: 1 Sam 19:22–24 (David, Samuel, Saul 2)

Wednesday of Week 6: 1 Sam 20:1–10 (David and Jonathan 2)

Thursday of Week 6: 1 Sam 20:11–24a (David and Jonathan 3)

Friday of Week 6: 1 Sam 20:24b–34 (David and Jonathan 4)

Saturday of Week 6: 1 Sam 20:35–42 (David and Jonathan 5)

Seventh Sunday in Ordinary Time: 1 Sam 21:1–8
    (David and Ahimelech)

Monday of Week 7 1 Sam 21:9–16 (David flees Saul 1)

Tuesday of Week 7: 1 Sam 22:1–10 (David flees Saul 2)

Wednesday of Week 7: 1 Sam 22:11–23 (David flees Saul 3)

Thursday of Week 7: 1 Sam 23:1–13 (Keilah)

Friday of Week 7: 1 Sam 23:14–24 (Ziphites 1)

Saturday of Week 7: 1 Sam 23:25–28 (Ziphites 2)

Eighth Sunday in Ordinary Time: 1 Sam 24:1–2, 22–23
    (David spares Saul)

Monday of Week 8: 1 Sam 25:1–13 (Samuel's death,
    Nabal and Abigail 1)

Tuesday of Week 8: 1 Sam 25:14–23 (Nabal and Abigail 2)

Wednesday of Week 8: 1 Sam 25:24–35 (Nabal and Abigail 3)

Thursday of Week 8: 1 Sam 25:36–43 (Nabal and Abigail 4)

Friday of Week 8: 1 Sam 26:1, 3–6, 10–11, 14–21, 24
    (Saul spared)

Saturday of Week 8: 1 Sam 27:1–12 (David's refuge)

Ninth Sunday in Ordinary Time: 1 Sam 28:1–7 (Philistines)

Monday of Week 9: 1 Sam 28:8–19 (witch of Endor)

Tuesday of Week 9: 1 Sam 28:20–25 (Saul's despair)

Wednesday of Week 9: 1 Sam 29:1–11 (David and Achish)

Thursday of Week 9: 1 Sam 30:1–16 (Ziglag)

Friday of Week 9: 1 Sam 30:17–25 (booty 1)

Saturday of Week 9: 1 Sam 30:26–31 (booty 2)

Tenth Sunday in Ordinary Time: 1 Sam 31:1–13 (Saul's death and burial)

Monday of Week 10: 2 Sam 1:5–10, 13–16 (Saul's death reported to David)

Tuesday of Week 10: 2 Sam 1:17–18, 20–22 (elegy)

Wednesday of Week 10: 2 Sam 2:1–7 (David declared king)

Thursday of Week 10: 2 Sam 2:8–16 (Ishbaal named king of Israel 1)

Friday of Week 10: 2 Sam 2:17–24 (Ishbaal named king of Israel 2)

Saturday of Week 10: 2 Sam 2:25—3:1 (Joab and Abner)

Eleventh Sunday in Ordinary Time: 2 Sam 3:2–11 (David, Ishbaal, Abner)

Monday of Week 11: 2 Sam 3:12–21 (Abner and David)

Tuesday of Week 11: 2 Sam 3:22–30 (death of Abner 1)

Wednesday of Week 11: 2 Sam 3:31–29 (death of Abner 2)

Thursday of Week 11: 2 Sam 4:1–7 (death of Ishbaal 1)

Friday of Week 11: 2 Sam 4:8–12 (death of Ishbaal 2)

Saturday of Week 11: 2 Sam 5:7–9, 11–12 (David captures Zion)

Twelfth Sunday in Ordinary Time: 2 Sam 5:13–25 (David's family, Philistines)

Monday of Week 12: 2 Sam 6:1–12a, 16 (ark brought to Jerusalem 1)

Tuesday of Week 12: 2 Sam 6:20–23 (ark brought to Jerusalem 2)

Wednesday of Week 12: 2 Sam 7:20–23, 25–28 (David's prayer)

Thursday of Week 12: 2 Sam 8:1–8 (David's wars 1)

Friday of Week 12: 2 Sam 8:9–18 (David's wars 2)

Saturday of Week 12: 23 Sam 9:1–13 (David and Meribaal)

Thirteenth Sunday in Ordinary Time: 2 Sam 10:1–14
   (Ammonites 1)

Monday of Week 13: 2 Sam 10:15–19 (Arameans)

Tuesday of Week 13: 2 Sam 11:11–12, 18–27 (David and Uriah)

Wednesday of Week 13: 2 Sam 12:7b–9, 18–25
   (David's punishment)

Thursday of Week 13: 2 Sam 12:26–31 (Ammonites 2)

Friday of Week 13: 2 Sam 13:1–22 (Ammon)

Saturday of Week 13: 2 Sam 13:23–28 (Absalom 1)

Fourteenth Sunday in Ordinary Time: 2 Sam 13:29–39
   (Absalom 2)

Monday of Week 14: 2 Sam 14:1–11 (Absolom 3)

Tuesday of Week 14: 2 Sam 14:12–20 (Absalom 4)

Wednesday of Week 14: 2 Sam 14:21–27 (Absalom 5)

Thursday of Week 14: 2 Sam 14:28–33 (Absalom 6)

Friday of Week 14: 2 Sam 15:1–12 (Absalom 7)

Saturday of Week 14: 2 Sam 15:15–23 (Absalom 8)

Fifteenth Sunday in Ordinary Time: 2 Sam 15:24–29, 31–37
   (Absalom 9)

Monday of Week 15: 2 Sam 16:1–4, 13–22 (Absalom 10)

Tuesday of Week 15: 2 Sam 16:23—17:14 (Absalom 11)

Wednesday of Week 15: 2 Sam 17:15–29 (Absalom 12)

Thursday of Week 15: 2 Sam 18:1–8, 11–13 (Absalom 13)

Friday of Week 15: 2 Sam 18:15–18 (Absalom 14)

Saturday of Week 15: 2 Sam 18:19–23, 25b–29 (Absalom 15)

Sixteenth Sunday in Ordinary Time: 2 Sam 19:4–15 (Absalom 16)

Monday of Week 16: 2 Sam 19:16–24 (David and Shimei)

Tuesday of Week 16: 2 Sam 19:25–31 (David and Meribaal)

Wednesday of Week 16: 2 Sam 19:32–41 (David and Barzillai 1)

Thursday of Week 16: 2 Sam 19:42–44 (David and Barzillai 2)

Friday of Week 16: 2 Sam 20:1–13 (Sheba 1)

Saturday of Week 16: 2 Sam 20:14–25 (Sheba 2)

Seventeenth Sunday in Ordinary Time: 2 Sam 21:1–14 (Gibeonites)

Monday of Week 17: 2 Sam 21:15–22 (Philistine wars)

Tuesday of Week 17: 2 Sam 22:1–16 (thanksgiving song 1)

Wednesday of Week 17: 2 Sam 22:1, 17–31 (thanksgiving song 2)

Thursday of Week 17: 2 Sam 22:32–51 (thanksgiving song 3)

Friday of Week 17: 2 Sam 23:1–7 (David's last words)

Saturday of Week 17: 2 Sam 23:8–39 (David's warriors)

Eighteenth Sunday in Ordinary Time: 2 Sam 24:1, 3–8, 18–25 (census)

Monday of Week 18: 1 Kgs 1:1–21 (David, Adonijah, Solomon)

Tuesday of Week 18: 1 Kgs 1:22–37 (Nathan, Bathsheba, Solomon)

Wednesday of Week 18: 1 Kgs 1:38–48 (Zadok, Nathan, Solomon 1)

Thursday of Week 18: 1 Kgs 1:49–53 (Zadok, Nathan, Silomon 2)

Friday of Week 18: 1 Kgs 2:5–9, 13–18 (David's instructions; Adonijah, Bathsheba)

Saturday of Week 18: 1 Kgs 2:19–27 (Bathsheba, Solomon, Abithar)

Nineteenth Sunday in Ordinary Time: 1 Kgs 2:28–46 (Joab and Solomon)

Monday of Week 19: 1 Kgs 3:1–3, 15 (Solomon's wisdom 1)

Tuesday of Week 19: 1 Kgs 3:16–28 (Solomon's wisdom 2)

Wednesday of Week 19: 1 Kgs 4:1–19 (Solomon's officers 1)

Thursday of Week 19: 1 Kgs 5:1–14 (Solomon's officers 2)

Friday of Week 19: 1 Kgs 5:15–24 (temple preparations 1)

Saturday of Week 19: 1 Kgs 5:25–32 (temple preparations 2)

Twentieth Sunday in Ordinary Time: 1 Kgs 6:1–13 (building temple 1)

Monday of Week 20: 1 Kgs 6:14–38 (building temple 2)

Tuesday of Week 20: 1 Kgs 7:1–12 (building palace)

Wednesday of Week 20: 1 Kgs 7:13–29 (finishing temple 1)

Thursday of Week 20: 1 Kgs 7:30–51 (finishing temple 2)

Friday of Week 20: Josh 1 Kgs 8:8, 14–21 (temple dedicated)

Saturday of Week 20: 1 Kgs 8:24–26, 31–40 (Solomon's prayer 1)

Twenty-first Sunday in Ordinary Time: 1 Kgs 8:44–54, 62–66 (Solomon's prayer 2)

Monday of Week 21: 1 Kgs 9:1–9 (the LORD appears to Solomon)

Tuesday of Week 21: 1 Kgs 9:10–23 (acts of Solomon 1)

Wednesday of Week 21: 1 Kgs 9:24–28 (acts of Solomon 2)

Thursday of Week 21: 1 Kgs 10:11–29 (Solomon's wealth)

Friday of Week 21 1 Kgs 11:1–3, 14–25 (Solomon's sins 1)

Saturday of Week 21: 1 Kgs 11:33–43 (Solomon's sins 2)

Twenty-second Sunday in Ordinary Time: 1 Kgs 12:1–17
(Rehoboam of Judah)

Monday of Week 22: 1 Kgs 12:18 20–25, 33 (Jeroboam of Israel)

Tuesday of Week 22: 1 Kgs 13:1–18 (Jeroboam in Bethel 1)

Wednesday of Week 22: 1 Kgs 13:19–32 (Jeroboam in Bethel 2)

Thursday of Week 22: 1 Kgs 14:1–11 (death of Abijah,
son of Jeroboam 1)

Friday of Week 22: 1 Kgs 14:7a, 12–20 (death of Abijah,
son of Jeroboam 2)

Saturday of Week 22: 1 Kgs 14:21:31 (Rehoboam)

Twenty-third Sunday in Ordinary Time: 1 Kgs 15:1–8
(Abijam of Judah)

Monday of Week 23: 1 Kgs 15:9–24 (Asa of Judah)

Tuesday of Week 23: 1 Kgs 15:25–32 (Nadab of Israel)

Wednesday of Week 23: 1 Kgs 15:33–34 (Basha of Israel 1)

Thursday of Week 23: 1 Kgs 16:1–7 (Basha of Israel 2)

Friday of Week 23: 1 Kgs 16:8–14 (Elah of Israel)

Saturday of Week 23: 1 Kgs 16:15–28 (Zimri, Omri of Israel)

Twenty-fourth Sunday in Ordinary Time: 1 Kgs 16:29–34
(Ahab of Israel)

Monday of Week 24: 1 Kgs 18:1–15 (Elijah and Ahab 1)

Tuesday of Week 24: 1 Kgs 18:16–19, 40 (Elijah and Ahab 2)

Wednesday of Week 24: 1 Kgs 20:1–21 (Ahab vs. Ben-hadad 1)

Thursday of Week 24: 1 Kgs 20:22–30 (Ahab vs. Ben-hadad 2)

Friday of Week 24: 1 Kgs 20:31–42 (Ahab vs. Ben-hadad 3)

Saturday of Week 24: 1 Kgs 22:1–17 (kings of Israel and Judah
    join forces 1)

Twenty-fifth Sunday in Ordinary Time: 1 Kgs 22:18–40
    (kings of Israel and Judah join forces 2)

Monday of Week 25: 1 Kgs 22:41–54 (Jehoshaphat of Judah,
    Ahaziah of Israel 1)

Tuesday of Week 25: 2 Kgs 1:1–18 (Ahaziah of Israel 2)

Wednesday of Week 25: 2 Kgs 2:2–5a, 15–25 (Elijah and Elisha)

Thursday of Week 25: 2 Kgs 3:1–14 (Joram of Israel 1)

Friday of Week 25: 2 Kgs 3:15–27 (Joram of Israel 2)

Saturday of Week 25: 2 Kgs 4:1–7, 12–13, 16b–17
    (oil for a widow)

Twenty-sixth Sunday in Ordinary Time: 2 Kgs 4:21b–31
    (the widow's son)

Monday of Week 26: 2 Kgs 4:38–41 (poisoned stew)

Tuesday of Week 26: 2 Kgs 5:18–24 (Naaman 1)

Wednesday of Week 26: 2 Kgs 5:25–27 (Naaman 2)

Thursday of Week 26: 2 Kgs 6:1–7 (lost ax)

Friday of Week 26: 2 Kgs 6:8–23 (Arameans)

Saturday of Week 26: 2 Kgs 6:24–33; 7:1–2 (Samaria under siege)

Twenty-seventh Sunday in Ordinary Time: 2 Kgs 7:3–13 (lepers)

Monday of Week 27: 2 Kgs 7:14–20 (siege ended)

Tuesday of Week 27: 2 Kgs 8:1–6 (famine)

Wednesday of Week 27: 2 Kgs 8:7–12 (death of Ben-hadad of Aram 1)

Thursday of Week 27: 1 Kgs 8:13–15 (death of Ben-hadad of Aram 2)

Friday of Week 27: 2 Kgs 8:16–24 (Jehoram of Judah)

Saturday of Week 27: 2 Kgs 8:25–29 (Amaziah of Judah)

Twenty-eighth Sunday in Ordinary Time: 2 Kgs 9:1–15a (Jehu of Israel 1)

Monday of Week 28: 2 Kgs 9:15b–26 (Joram of Israel)

Tuesday of Week 28: 2 Kgs 9:27–37 (Jezebel)

Wednesday of Week 28: 2 Kgs 10:1–11 (Ahab's descendants)

Thursday of Week 28: 2 Kgs 10:12–17 (Ahaziah's kinsmen)

Friday of Week 28: 2 Kgs 10:18–27 (Baal's temple, Jehu of Israel 2)

Saturday of Week 28: 2 Kgs 10:28–36 (Baal's temple, Jehu of Israel 3)

Twenty-ninth Sunday in Ordinary Time: 2 Kgs 11:5–8, 19 (Athaliah, Joash)

Monday of Week 29: 2 Kgs 12:1–9 (Joash of Judah 1)

Tuesday of Week 29: 2 Kgs 12:10–22 (Joash of Judah 2)

Wednesday of Week 29: 2 Kgs 13:1–9 (Jehoahaz of Israel)

Thursday of Week 29: 2 Kgs 13:10–19 (Jehoash of Israel)

Friday of Week 29: 2 Kgs 13:20–25 (death of Elisha)

Saturday of Week 29: 2 Kgs 14:1–16 (Amaziah of Judah 1)

Thirtieth Sunday in Ordinary Time: 2 Kgs 14:17–22 (Amaziah of Judah 2)

Monday of Week 30: 2 Kgs 14:23–29 (Jeroboam II of Israel)

Tuesday of Week 30: 2 Kgs 15:1–16 (Azariah of Judah, Zechariah of Israel, Shallum of Israel)

Wednesday of Week 30: 2 Kgs 15:17–31 (Menahem of Israel, Pekahiah of Israel, Pekah of Israel)

Thursday of Week 30: 2 Kgs 15:32–38 (Jotham of Judah)

Friday of Week 30: 2 Kgs 16:1–9 (Ahaz of Judah 1)

Saturday of Week 30: 2 Kgs 16:10–20 (Ahaz of Judah 2)

Thirtieth-first Sunday in Ordinary Time: 2 Kgs 17:1–4, 9–12, 15b–17 (Hoshea of Israel)

Monday of Week 31: 2 Kgs 17:19–28 (Judah 1)

Tuesday of Week 31: 2 Kgs 17:29–41 (Judah 2)

Wednesday of Week 31: 2 Kgs 18:1–12 (Hezekiah of Judah)

Thursday of Week 31: 2 Kgs 18:13–22 (Sennacherib 1)

Friday of Week 31: 2 Kgs 18:23–37 (Sennacherib 2)

Saturday of Week 31: 2 Kgs 19:1–9, 12–13 (Hezekiah and Isaiah 1)

Thirty-second Sunday in Ordinary Time: 2 Kgs 19:22–30, 37 (Hezekiah and Isaiah 2)

Monday of Week 32: 2 Kgs 20:7–21 (Hezekiah's illness)

Tuesday of Week 32: 2 Kgs 21:1–18 (Manasseh of Judah)

Wednesday of Week 32: 2 Kgs 21:19–26 (Amon of Judah)

Thursday of Week 32: 2 Kgs 22:1–7, 14–20 (Josiah of Judah 1)

Friday of Week 32: 2 Kgs 23:4–7 (Josiah of Judah 2)

Saturday of Week 32: 2 Kgs 23:8–18 (Josiah of Judah 3)

Thirty-third Sunday in Ordinary Time: 2 Kgs 23:19–30
(Josiah of Judah 4)

Monday of Week 33: 2 Kgs 23:31–37 (Jehoahaz,
Jehoiakim of Judah)

Tuesday of Week 33: 2 Kgs 24:1–7 (Nebuchadnezzar)

Wednesday of Week 33: 2 Kgs 24:18–20; 25:13–17 (Zedekiah 1)

Thursday of Week 33: 2 Kgs 25:18–21 (Zedekiah 2)

Friday of Week 33: 2 Kgs 25:22–26 (Gedaliah 1)

Saturday of Week 33: 2 Kgs 25:27–30 (Gedaliah 2)

Solemnity of Christ the King (Thirty-fourth Sunday in Ordinary
Time): 2 Chr 36:2–4 or Ezra 1:1–4 (Jehoahaz of Judah and
Jehoiakim of Judah; decree of Cyrus 1)

Monday of Week 34: 2 Chr 36:5–8 or Ezra 1:5–11 (Jehoiakim of
Judah, Nebuchadnezzar; decree of Cyrus 2)

Tuesday of Week 34: 2 Chr 36:9–13 or Ezra 2:1–12
(Jehoiachin, Zedekiah; census 1)

Wednesday of Week 34: 2 Chr 36:15–16 or Ezra 2:2b, 13–35
(dissolution of Judah 1; census 2)

Thursday of Week 34: 2 Chr 36:17–18 or Ezra 2:36–42
(dissolution of Judah 2; census 3)

Friday of Week 34: 2 Chr 36:19–21 or Ezra 2:43–54
(destruction of the temple; census 4)

Saturday of Week 34: 2 Chr 36:22–23 or Ezra 2:55–70
(declaration of Cyrus; census 5)

The *Lectionary* and the *Bible*

9

Miscellaneous Alternatives

Because there are fifty-two gospel pericopes not included in the Lectionary's Sunday Cycles A, B, and C nor in its Weekday Year I or II, what follows are alternative sets of texts that can be used during fifty-two consecutive days (organized in eight weeks of texts) or used for 52 Sundays. Based on the principle of continuous or semi-continuous readings, the First Reading comes from the OT (A) books of Judith and Esther; the Second Reading comes from Romans, 1 Corinthians, and 2 Corinthians, passages not in the current Lectionary. A single Responsorial Psalm is provided for passages from the book of Judith, and a single Responsorial Psalm is provided for passages from the book of Esther. Other Responsorial Psalms can be found in the Lectionary (pars 173,

174, 703, 709, 715, 721, 727, 733, 739). Alleluia Verses before the gospel can be chosen from those in the Lectionary (pars 163, 192, 201, 211, 218, 223, 303, 304, 509, 705, 711, 717, 723, 729, 735, 741). The following Miscellaneous Alternatives can be considered an alternate set of texts that can be used by individuals, assigned by the administration of a church, or left to the choice of a pastor of a parish. However, it must be noted that both the First Reading and the Second Reading are semi-continuous. The parentheses after each entry contain a word or phrase that describes each biblical passage above it. Thus, Sunday of the First Week presents Jdt 1:1–16 (Assyria vs. Medes); Rom 1:8–15 (thanksgiving); and Matt 4:18–22 (call of disciples).

Common Responsorial Psalm for First Readings from the book of Judith (First through Fifth Week):

(16:16) R./ Sing a new song to the LORD.

Jdt 16:1, 2, 3, 5–6

First Week

(1) Sunday: Jdt 1:1–16; Rom 1:8–15; Matt 4:18–22

(Assyria vs. Medes; thanksgiving; call of disciples)

(2) Monday: Jdt 2:1–13; Rom 1:26–32; Matt 12:9-13

(Nebuchadnezzar and Holofernes; God handed over; man with withered hand)

(3) Tuesday: Jdt 2:14–28; Rom 2:12–29; Matt 12:22–32

(Holofernes' campaign; judgment by interior law and Mosaic law; Jesus and Beelzebul)

(4) Wednesday: Jdt 3:1–10; Rom 3:1–20, 31; Matt 12:33–37

(Submission; answers to objections; a tree and its fruit)

(5) Thursday: Jdt 4:1–8; Rom 4:9-12, 15; Matt 12:43–45

(Israel's defense; blessings; unclean spirit)

(6) Friday: Jdt 4:9–15; Rom 5:16; 6:1; 7:1–17, 25b; Matt 15:3–9

(Prayer and penance; freedom; tradition)

(7) Saturday: Jdt 5:1–16; Rom 9:6–24; Matt 15:15–20

(Israelite history 1; God's choice; parables explained)

Second Week

(8) Sunday: Jdt 5:17–23; Rom 9:25–33; Matt 16:1–4

(Israelite history 2; prophets; sign)

(9) Monday: Jdt 6:1–9; Rom 10:1–7, 19–21; Matt 16:5–12

(Holofernes' reply; righteousness; leaven)

(10) Tuesday: Jdt 6:10–20; Rom 11:2b–10; Matt 18:6–9

(Achior in Bethulia; remnant chosen by grace; temptation to sin)

(11) Wednesday: Jdt 7:1–7; Rom 11:13–24; Matt 20:29–34

(Siege of Bethulia 1; Gentiles saved; two blind men healed)

(12) Thursday: Jdt 7:8–18; Rom 12:19—13:7; Matt 21:12–17

(Siege of Bethulia 2; revenge, authority; temple cleansed)

(13) Friday: Jdt 7:19–32; Rom 14:1–6; Matt 21:18–22

(Siege of Bethulia 3; opinions; fig tree cursed)

(14) Saturday: Jdt 8:1, 9–16; Rom 14:13–23; Matt 22:23–33

(Judith 1; walk in conscience; resurrection)

Third Week

(15) Sunday: Jdt 8:17–27; Rom 15:1–3, 10–13; Matt 22:41–45

(Judith 2; patience; David's son)

(16) Monday: Jdt 8:28–35; Rom 15:22–33; Matt 23:33–39

(Uzziah, plans; Paul's plans, need for prayer; scribes
   and Pharisees)

(17) Tuesday: Jdt 9:1–14; Rom 16:1–2, 10–15; Matt 24:1–3

(Judith's prayer; greetings; destruction of the temple)

(18) Wednesday: Jdt 10:1–10; Rom 16:17–21; Matt 24:15–28

(Judith prepares for battle; greetings; tribulation)

(19) Thursday: Jdt 10:11–23; 1 Cor 1:14; 3:12–15; Matt 24:29–36

(Judith meets Holofernes; building; coming of the Son of man)

(20) Friday: Jdt 11:1–15; 1 Cor 4:6a, 16–21; Matt 26:1–13

(Judith and Holofernes 1; imitate Paul; anointing at Bethany

(21) Saturday: Jdt 11:16–23; Cor 5:9–13a, 15b–16; Mark 13:1–13

(Judith and Holofernes 2; associates; temple destruction)

Fourth Week

(22) Sunday: Jdt 12:1–9; 1 Cor 6:12–13a, 15b–16; Mark 13:14–23

(The plan 1; sexual immorality; tribulation)

(23) Monday: Jdt 12:10–19; 1 Cor 7:1–16; Luke 3:23–38

(The plan 2; marriage; Jesus' genealogy)

(24) Tuesday: Jdt 13:1–10a; 1 Cor 7:17–24; Luke 8:22–25

(The plan 3; follow the call; storm at sea)

(25) Wednesday: Jdt 13:10b–17; 1 Cor 7:36–40; Luke 8:26–39

(Return to Bethulia; virginity; Gerasene demoniac)

(26) Thursday: Jdt 14:1–10; 1 Cor 8:1, 8–10; Luke 8:40–56

(Holofernes' head displayed; food; Jairus' daughter, woman
   with hemorrhage)

(27) Friday: Jdt 14:11–19; 1 Cor 9:1–15, 20–22a; Luke 9:37–43

(Achior circumcised; rights, all things to all; healing a boy)

(28) Saturday: Jdt 15:1–10; 1 Cor 10:7–9, 13, 23–30;
    Luke 11:33–36

(Word spreads; warnings, seek the good; light)

Fifth Week

(29) Sunday: Jdt 15:11—16:6; 1 Cor 11:2–16; Luke 12:22–31

(Assyrian camp plundered; Christ is the head; depend on God)

(30) Monday: Jdt 16:7–17; 1 Cor 11: 27–32; Luke 16:16–18

(Hymn; the Lord's supper; sayings about law, divorce)

(31) Tuesday: Jdt 16:18–25; 1 Cor 12:1–3a; Luke 18:15–17

(Thanksgiving in Jerusalem; spiritual gifts; children and
    the kingdom)

Common Responsorial Psalm for First Readings from the book
    of Esther (Fifth through Eighth Week):

R./ The LORD saves his people.

Ps 13:2, 4, 6

(32) Wednesday: Esth A:1–17; 1 Cor 14:1–12; Luke 18:18–23

(Mordecai; prophecy; rich official)

(33) Thursday: Esth 1:1–9; 1 Cor 14:13–25; Luke 18:24–30

(The king's banquet; interpretation of tongues, function of gifts;
    riches)

(34) Friday: Esth 1:10–22; 1 Cor 14:26–40; Luke 18:31–34

(Vashti; order; passion prediction)

(35) Saturday: Esth 2:1–10; 1 Cor 15:29–34; Luke 20:1–8

(Search for a new queen; practical arguments; Jesus' authority)

Sixth Week

(36) Sunday: Esth 2:11–21; 1 Cor 15:38–41, 50; Luke 20:9–19

(Esther chosen queen; resurrection; tenant farmers)

(37) Monday: Esth 3:1–13; 1 Cor 16:1–12; Luke 20:20–26

(Haman; collection; paying taxes)

(38) Tuesday: Esth B:1–7; 1 Cor 16:13–24; Luke 20:41–47

(Haman's letter; greetings; David's son)

(39) Wednesday: Esth 4:1–15; 2 Cor 1:8–17; Luke 21:37–38

(Mordecai seeks Esther's help; afflictions, boasting; ministry
in Jerusalem)

(40) Thursday: Esth C:1–11; 2 Cor 2:1–13; Luke 22:1–6

(Mordecai's prayer; change of plans, pain; conspiracy)

(41) Friday: Esth C:12–13, 17–22, 26–30; 2 Cor 2:14–17;
Luke 22:7–13, 23–24

(Esther's prayer; new covenant; preparation for Passover)

(42) Saturday: Esth D:1–15; 2 Cor 3:12–14; John 2:12

(The king receives Esther 1; hope; to Capernaum)

Seventh Week

(43) Sunday: Esth 5:1–8; 2 Cor 5:2–5, 11–13; John 4:1–3

(The king receives Esther 2; tent, fear of the Lord; baptizing)

(44) Monday: Esth 5:9–14; 2 Cor 6:11—7:3; John 6:70–71

(Esther reveals Haman's plot; holiness; chosen)

(45) Tuesday: Esth 6:1–13; 2 Cor 7:4–16; John 7:2–9, 11–13

(Mordecai rewarded; Macedonia; feast of tabernacles)

(46) Wednesday: Esth 6:14—7:10; 2 Cor 8:16–24; John 7:19–24

(Esther's banquet; Titus; law)

(47) Thursday: Esth 8:1–12, 13–17; 2 Cor 9:1–5; John 7:31–33

(The king favors Esther and Mordecai; gift; belief, arrest)

(48) Friday: Esth E:1–16; 2 Cor 10:1–16; John 8:43–50

(The king's letter 1; Paul; understanding)

(49) Saturday: Esth E:17–24; 12 Cor 11:12–17; John 12:17–19

(The king's letter 2; false apostles; consequences of
Lazarus' raising)

Eighth Week

(50) Sunday: Esth 9:1–17; 2 Cor 11:19–21a, 30–33; John
12:36b–43

(Jewish enemies defeated 1; Paul's labors; belief and unbelief)

(51) Monday: Esth 9:18–32; 2 Cor 12:11–21; John 15:22–25

(Jewish enemies defeated 2; concern for the church; hate)

(52) Tuesday: Esth 10:1–3; F:1–10; 2 Cor 13:1–10; John 20:30–31

(The king's tribute, Mordecai's dream; living in faith;
first conclusion)

The *Lectionary* and the *Bible*

10

Solemnity Alternatives

In the Roman Catholic Lectionary, the highest rank of any liturgical day is the solemnity. Below are listed the dates and the solemnities that occur during the liturgical year. The biblical texts assigned by the Lectionary are listed in bold (**Texts**) and suggestions for other biblical texts are listed in italics (*Alternative Texts*). The texts assigned by the Lectionary are in the order in which they appear in the Lectionary; the list of multiple texts connected by *or* indicate that there are three cycles of texts available. The suggestions for other biblical texts are in the order in which they are found in the Bible. Some of the alternative texts may need to be edited.

January 1: The Blessed Virgin Mary, Mother of God

Texts: Num 6:22–27; Gal 4:4–7; Luke 2:16–21

Alternative Texts: Gen 21:22–24, 33–34; Num 29:1–6; Deut 33:1–5, 26–29; 1 Sam 3:11–18; Jdt 12:1–4, 15—13:8; Rom 1:8–15; Gal 3:15–21

January 6: The Epiphany of the Lord

Texts: Isa 60:1–6; Eph 3:2–3a, 5–6; Matt 2:1–12

Alternative Texts: Exod 20:18–26; Exod 33:18–23; 1 Sam 3:11–18; 2 Kgs 4:1–7; Luke 8:22–25; Luke 8:26–39; Luke 8:40–56; Luke 9:37–43; John 4:1–3; John 12:36b–43; John 20:30–31; Rom 11:13–24; Heb 6:1–9

March 19: St. Joseph, Husband of the Blessed Virgin Mary

Texts: 2 Sam 7:4–5a, 12–14a, 16; Rom 4:13, 16–18, 22; Matt 1:16, 18–21, 24a or Luke 2:41–51a

Alternative Texts: Deut 25:5–10; Ruth 3:1–15; Ruth 4: 1–12; Tob 4:1–6; Esth 3:1–7; Sir 14:20–27; Luke 12:22–31; Rom 4:9–12; Rom 9:1–17

March 25: The Annunciation of the Lord

Texts: Isa 7:10–14; 8:10; Heb 19:4–10; Luke 1:26–38

Alternative Texts: 1 Sam 2:18–21; 1 Kgs 1:22–35; 2 Chr 7:1–6; Amos 1:1–2; 2:4–5; Luke 11:33–36; Rom 9:6–33

Holy Thursday: Evening Mass of the Lord's Supper

Texts: Exod 12:1–8, 11–14; 1 Cor 11:23–26; John 13:1–15

Alternative Texts: Num 29:7–11; Deut 16:1–8; Josh 4:1–9; 2 Chr 30:14–27; Esth 5:1–13; Esth 7:1–10; Wis 16:16–21; Matt 26:1–13; Luke 22:1–13; 1 Cor 11:27–32

Good Friday: The Lord's Passion

Texts: Isa 52:13—53:12; Heb 4:14–16; 5:7–9; John 18:1—19:42

Alternative Texts: Deut 32:45-52; 2 Chr 18:28-34; Esth 4:1-2, 4-16; I Macc 2:1-14; 2 Macc 5:11-20; Job 16:1, 6-22; 17:1; Isa 51:17-23; Jer 19:1-13; Matt 23:33—24:2, 15-16; Luke 20:9-19

The Resurrection of the Lord

Texts: The Easter Vigil: Gen 1:1—2:2 or 1:1, 26-31a; Gen 22:1-18 or 22:1-2, 9a, 10-13, 15-18; Exod 14:15—15:1; Isa 54:5-14; Isa 55:1-11; Bar 3:9-15, 32—4:4; Ezek 36:16-17a, 18-28; Rom 6:3-11; Matt 28:1-10 or Mark 16:1-7; or Luke 24:1-12

Alternative Texts: Creation and Water: Exod 15:22-27; Exod 17:1-7; Num 20:2-13; 2 Kgs 5:1-27; Job 38:1—39:30; Prov 8:22-31; Sir 16:24—17:11; Sir 30:12-35; Sir 43:1-35; Rev 22:1-5;

Exodus and Passover: Num 9:1-5, 15-23; Deut 11:1-9; Deut 16:1-8; Josh 3:1-17; Josh 4:1-24; Josh 5:1-15; Neh 9:1-37; Wis 18:1—19:22;

Patriarchs: Gen 18:1-15 (Abraham); Gen 18:16—19:29 (Abraham and Lot); Gen 25:19-34 (Esau and Jacob); Gen 27:1-45 (Esau and Jacob); Gen 28:1—22 (Jacob); Gen 32:23-33 (Jacob); Gen 35:9-15 (Jacob); Gen 37:1-36 (Joseph); Gen 41:1-46 (Joseph) Gen 46:1-7, 26-34; 47:1-12 (Jacob); Exod 3:1—4:17 (Moses and Aaron); Exod 33:18-23; 34:1-9, 28 (Moses); Num 22:1—24:25 (Balaam); Deut 31:1—32:44 (Joshua); 1 Sam 16:1-13 (David); 2 Sam 11:1—12:25 (David); 2 Macc 6:18-31 (Eleazar); 2 Macc 7:1-42 (Mother and Seven Sons); Sir 44:1, 19-23 (Abraham);

Miscellaneous: Exod 32:1-35 (Golden Calf); Num 6:1-21 (Nazarites); Num 11:1-15 (Manna); Num 11:16-30 (Seventy Elders); Num 11:31-35 (Quail); Num 13:1—14:45 (Reconnoitering Canaan); Num 19:1-22 (Heifer Ashes); Num 21:4-9 (Bronze Serpent); 2 Sam 6:1—7:29 (Ark brought to Jerusalem); Wis 10:1-21 (History of Wisdom);

Prophets: 1 Kgs 17:1-6 (Elijah); 1 Kgs 17:7-24 (Elijah); 1 Kgs 18:1-46 (Elijah); 1 Kgs 21: 1-29 (Elijah); 2 Kgs 4:1-7 (Elisha);

2 Kgs 4:8–37 (Elisha); Isa 6:1–13 (Isaiah); Jer 1:4–19 (Jeremiah); Ezek 2:1–15 (Ezekiel); Ezek 37:15–28 (Ezekiel); Hos 2:1—3:5 (Hosea); Amos 7:10—8:14 (Amos); Jonas 1:1—2:1, 11 (Jonah); Jonah 3:1—4:11 (Jonah);

<u>Faith and Resurrection</u>: Rom 3:21–31; Rom 4:1–25; Rom 5:12–20; Rom 14:7–9; 1 Cor 15:1–11; 1 Cor 15:12–28; 1 Cor 15:35–58; Eph 1:11–23; Eph 2:1–10; 1 Thess 4:13–18; 5:1–11; Titus 2:11–14; Titus 3:4–8; Heb 11:1—12:4; 1 Pet 3:13–22; Rev 21:1–7, 9b–27

Texts: Easter Day: Acts 10:34a, 37–43; Col 3:1–4 or 1 Cor 5:6b–8; John 20:1–9

Alternative Texts: Num 9:1–8; Num 9:9–14; Num 33:1–56; Deut 9:1–6; 2 Macc 10:1–8; Wis 11:1–14; Wis 18:1–4; Obad 1:17–21; Matt 22:23–33

Pentecost

Texts: Vigil: Gen 11:1–9; Exod 19:3–8a, 16–20b; Ezek 37:1–14; Joel 3:1–5; Rom 8:22–27; John 7:37–39

Day: Acts 2:1–11; 1 Cor 12:3b–7, 12–13 or Gal 5:16–25 or Rom 8:8–17; John 20:19–23 or 15:26–27; 16:12–15 or 14:15–16, 23b–26

Alternative Texts: Exod 24:12–18; Num 9:15–23; Num 28:26–31; Deut 5:1–11; Deut 16:9–12; Josh 1:1–9

Sunday after Pentecost: The Most Holy Trinity

Texts: Exod 34:4b–6, 8–9 or Deut 4:32–34, 39–40 or Prov 8:22–31; 2 Cor 13:11–13 or Rom 8:14–17 or Rom 5:1–5; John 3:16–18 or Matt 28:16–20 or John 16:12–15

Alternative Texts: Josh 23:1–13; 1 Sam 29:1–12; 1 Sam 20:35—21:1; 2 Sam 6:1–11; 1 Sam 6:16, 20–23; 1 Chr 13:1–14; 1 Chr 15:1–2, 25–29; Job 35:1; 36:22–33; Prov 3:1–12; Prov 8:1–21; Prov 9:10–12; Wis 8:2–9; Sir 1:12–18; Sir 24:8–11, 17–22; Isa 44:6–8; Mal 3:8–12; Phil 1:1–6

Sunday after Trinity Sunday: The Most Holy Body and Blood of Christ

Texts: Deut 8:2–3, 14b–16a or Exod 24:3–8 or Gen 14:18–20; 1 Cor 10:16–17 or Heb 9:11–15 or 1 Cor 11:23–26; John 6:51–58 or Mark 14:12–16, 22–26 or Luke 9:11b–17

Alternative Texts: Lev 17:1–6, 11–12; Lev 21:1–6, 10–12; Num 11:18–23; Num 11:31–34; Num 28:16–25; Deut 12:15–19; Deut 12:20–28

Friday after the Second Sunday after Pentecost: The Most Sacred Heart of Jesus

Texts: Deut 7:6–11 or Hos 11:1, 3–4, 8c–9 or Ezek 34:11–16; 1 John 4:7–16 or Eph 3:8–12, 14–19 or Rom 5:5b–11; Matt 11:25–30 or John 19:31–37 or Luke 15:3–7

Alternative Texts: Deut 11:1–9; Josh 2:1–14; 1 Kgs 3:16–27; John 7:19–24, 31–33

June 24: The Nativity of St. John the Baptist

Texts: Vigil: Jer 1:4–10; 1 Pet 1:8–12; Luke 1:5–17

Day: Isa 49:1–6; Acts 13:22–26; Luke 1:57–66, 80

Alternative Texts: Num 6:1–8; Num 6:13–21; Num 27:12–22; Judg 6:1–10; Judg 13:9–23; Job 2:1–10; Job 9:1; 10:2–12, 18–22; Job 12:1; 14:1–10; Jer 20:14–18; Luke 3:19; Luke 20:1–8

June 29: SS. Peter and Paul, Apostles

Texts: Vigil: Acts 3:1–10; Gal 1:11–20; John 21:15–19

Day: Acts 12:1–11; 2 Tim 4:6–8, 17–18; Matt 16:13–19

Alternative Texts: Num 25:10–13; 1 Sam 18:1–5; Tob 4:18–19; Tob 5:4–14; Job 4:1, 12–21; Job 6:1, 8–13, 24–30; Prov 22:1–12; Zech 1:7–17; Acts 5:1–11; Acts 8:9–13, 18–25; Acts 10:1–24a, 27–32; Acts 12:12–19; Acts 14:1–4; 15:36–41; Acts 17:1–14;

Acts 20:1–16; Acts 22:22–29; 1 Cor 9:1–12a; 2 Cor 1:8–11; 2 Cor 2:14–17; 2 Cor 10:1–16

August 15: The Assumption of the Blessed Virgin Mary

Texts: Vigil: 1 Chr 15:3–4, 15–16; 16:1–2; 1 Cor 15:54b–57; Luke 11:27–28

Day: Rev 11:19a; 12:1–6a, 10ab; 1 Cor 15:20–27; Luke 1:39–56

Alternative Texts: Lev 10:1–5; 1 Sam 28:7–17; 2 Kgs 2:11–12; 2 Chr 9:1–9; Eccl 9:1–10; 2 Cor 5:2–5

November 1: All Saints

Texts: Rev 7:2–4, 9–14; 1 John 3:1–3; Matt 5:1–12a

Alternative Texts: Deut 1:6–8; Josh 6:1–11; Josh 6:12–19; Josh 6:20–25; 1 Chr 11:4–9; Neh 12:27–30; Tob 4:7–11, 16–17; Ezek 15:1–6; Ezek 19:1–9; Ezek 19:10–14; Mic 4:5–8; Luke 14:34–35; Luke 18:18–30; Heb 11:20–31; Rev 10:1–7; Rev 15:5–8

Last Sunday of the Liturgical Year: Our Lord Jesus Christ the King

Texts: Ezek 34:11–12, 15–17 or Dan 7:13–14 or 2 Sam 5:1–3; 1 Cor 15:20–26, 28 or Rev 1:5–8 or Col 1:12–20; Matt 25:31–46 or John 18:33b–37 or Luke 23:35–43

Alternative Texts: Lev 16:5–22; Deut 17:14–20; 1 Sam 8:1–9; 1 Sam 9:26b—10:1ab; 1 Sam 15:1–9; 2 Sam 2:1–7; 1 Chr 11:1–3; Isa 33:17–24; Dan 4:1–15; Dan 4:16–24, 31–32; Zech 10:3b–12; Rev 1:14–16; Rev 3:7–13; Rev 19:11–16

December 8: The Immaculate Conception of the Blessed Virgin Mary

Texts: Gen 3:9–15, 20; Eph 1:3–6, 11–12; Luke 1:26–38

Alternative Texts: Neh 8:13–18; Song 4:1–7; Song 4:10–11; Song 4:12–16

December 25: The Nativity of the Lord

Texts: Vigil: Isa 62:1–5; Acts 13:16–17, 22–25; Matt 1:1–25 or 1:18–25

Night: Isa 9:1–6; Titus 2:11–14; Luke 2:1–14

Dawn: Isa 62:11–12; Titus 3:4–7; Luke 2:15–20

Day: Isa 52:7–10; Heb 1:1–6; John 1:1–18 or 1:1–5, 9–14

Alternative Texts: Judg 3:7–11; Judg 3:12–25; Judg 3:26–31; Judg 4:1–9; Judg 4:10–16; Judg 4:17–24; Judg 5:1–5; Judg 5:6–13; Judg 5:14–22; Judg 5:23–31; 1 Kgs 6:11–13; 1 Kgs 7:14–21; 1 Chr 2:1–17; 1 Chr 3: 1–9; 1 Chr 3:10–24; 2 Chr 3:1–14; Eccl 11:3–6; Wis 6:22—7:6; Sir 43:1–12; Heb 3:1–6

11

The Lectionary and the Liturgical Year

While this book is about the Roman Catholic Lectionary, the Lectionary is dictated by the liturgical year. In other words, the liturgical year dictates what is in the Lectionary from the Bible. Therefore, the liturgical year needs to be refined for modern people. As early as December 4, 1963, in the "Appendix" to the "Constitution on the Sacred Liturgy," Pope Paul VI notes that there was no objection "if the feast of Easter were assigned to a particular Sunday of the Gregorian Calendar."[1] Likewise, there was no opposition to the introduction of a perpetual calendar.

---

1. "Appendix."

Over the course of the intervening years, the suggested date for Easter has been the second Sunday of April, regardless of the date. Setting the date for Easter as the second Sunday of April every year would streamline the most moveable celebration of the church. As it currently stands, Easter is calculated as the first Sunday after the first full moon after the Spring Equinox. That means that, depending on the moon, Easter may fall between March 21 and April 25. Most people today do not use the moon to calculate any Christian feasts! With Easter fixed on the second Sunday of Easter (no matter what that date may be), Ash Wednesday, the beginning of Lent, would be standardized as beginning with the Wednesday during the fourth week of February. Palm Sunday of the Passion of the Lord would be the first Sunday of April.

In general, with the establishment of the second Sunday of April as Easter every year, Pentecost, the end of the Easter Season, would be the first Sunday of June, followed by Trinity Sunday on the second Sunday of June, the Solemnity of the Body and Blood of Christ on the third Sunday of June, and the resumption of the Sundays of Ordinary Time on the fourth Sunday of June. Every year, there would be six Sundays of Ordinary Time before Ash Wednesday.

Further standardization of Advent and Christmas would also help streamline the Lectionary. If Christmas were celebrated on the fourth Sunday of December (no matter the date), Advent would begin four Sundays before it. Thus, the Season of Advent would always be four weeks long, either beginning the last Sunday of November or the first Sunday of December. Christmas Day would always be the fourth Sunday of December, no matter the date. The Christmas Season would consist of the Feast of the Holy Family marked on the Sunday between Christmas and January 1 (or January 30 if there is no Sunday), Epiphany on the first Sunday of January (no matter the date), and the Baptism of the Lord on the second Sunday of January (no matter the date). There would be two full weeks of the Christmas Season. Thus, the Sundays of Ordinary Time would begin on the third Sunday of January (with the first week of Ordinary Time starting on the Monday after the

Baptism of the Lord). The current 34 Sundays of Ordinary Time would be reduced to 31 weeks of Ordinary Time; Sundays and weeks which are now omitted (depending on the organization of the civil calendar) would not be needed, as the numbering of weeks before Lent would always be six, and after Pentecost (which ends the Easter Season) would continue with week 7 to 31. The last Sunday of Ordinary Time remains Christ the King, with the Sunday following it being the First Sunday of Advent.

The United States civil calendar solved most of its moveable holidays by putting them on Mondays. Thus, no matter what day Martin Luther King's birthday occurs, it is always celebrated on the third Monday of January. No matter what day Washington's Birthday occurs, it is always celebrated on President's Day, the third Monday of February. Even though Memorial Day is May 30, it is marked on the last Monday of May, no matter what the date. Churches using a Lectionary need to learn a lesson from the way the civil calendar has been adjusted to meet the needs of modern people. Some special days can be marked by those who observe the day as a holiday. Placing the holiday on the third Monday of a month or the last Monday of a month makes it easier to be remembered and celebrated by those who desire to observe it.

To those who would object to setting the second Sunday of April as Easter every year and the fourth Sunday of December as Christmas every year, we can say that we have no historical evidence for keeping the dates as is. Calculating Easter according to the moon and the equinox had nothing to do historically with the date of Jesus' resurrection. Likewise, establishing December 25 as the observance of his Nativity has nothing to do with the date when he was born. We do not know when he rose from the dead or when he was born. The way to calculate Easter was based on the way the Jews calculate Passover. And the choice of December 25 was in opposition to the Roman holiday of *Sol Invictus*, a celebration of the return of the sun, longer days after the December 21 Winter Solstice.

The standardization of the liturgical calendar would facilitate the standardization of the Lectionary that serves the liturgical calendar.

Instead of trying to get other religious groups to agree to move Easter to the second Sunday of April and Christmas to the fourth Sunday of December, the Roman Catholic Church needs just to do it. Other religious groups will follow. After the Roman Catholic Church began to mark Sunday on Saturday evening, almost every religious group began a Saturday afternoon or evening service. They were not consulted, but it didn't take long for them to follow. Also, once the Roman Catholic Church issued its Lectionary, it didn't take long for other religious groups to adopt it and alter it to fit their needs. In those ways, the Roman Catholic Church can take a leadership role among other religious groups. Yes, there will be some who will not change, but over time all will see the wisdom of streamlining the liturgical year and the Lectionary that accompanies it.

The *Lectionary* and the *Bible*

Bibliography

"Appendix: A Declaration of the Second Ecumenical Council of the Vatican on Revision of the Calendar." Constitution on the Sacred Liturgy, Sacrosanctum Concilium. (December 4, 1963) https://www.vatican.va/archive/hist_councils/ii_vatican_council/documents/vat-ii_const_19631204_sacrosanctum-concilium_en.html.

"Appendix II: Table of Readings." In *Lectionary for Mass: Volume I: Sundays, Solemnities, Feasts of the Lord and the Saints*. New Jersey: Catholic Book, 1998.

"Appendix III: Table of Responsorial Psalms and Canticles." In *Lectionary for Mass: Volume I: Sundays, Solemnities, Feasts of the Lord and the Saints*. New Jersey: Catholic Book, 1998.

Flannery, Austin, ed. "The Constitution on the Sacred Liturgy." In *Vatican Council II: The Conciliar and Post Conciliar Documents*. Northport, NY: Costello, 1975.

———. "Dogmatic Constitution on Divine Revelation." In *Vatican Council II: The Conciliar and Post Conciliar Documents*. Northport, NY: Costello, 1975.

"Introduction." In *Lectionary for Mass: Volume I: Sundays, Solemnities, Feasts of the Lord and the Saints*. New Jersey: Catholic Book, 1998.

Meyer, Michael A. "The Preacher as a Witness to the Sacramentality of the Word in Liturgy." *Worship* 98:1 (2024) 66–75.

O'Day, Gail R., and David Petersen, eds. *The Access Bible: New Revised Standard Version with the Apocryphal/Deuterocanonical Books, Updated Edition.* New York: Oxford University Press, 2011.

Schuller, Eileen. "The Bible in the Lectionary." In *The Catholic Bible Personal Study Edition*, edited by Jean Marie Hiesberger, 1769–76. New York: Oxford, 2007.

Turner, Paul. *Words without Alloy: A Biography of the Lectionary for Mass.* Collegeville, MN: Liturgical Academic, 2022.

Recent Books by Mark G. Boyer
Published by Wipf & Stock

Nature Spirituality: Praying with Wind, Water, Earth, Fire

A Spirituality of Ageing

Weekday Saints: Reflections on Their Scriptures

Human Wholeness: A Spirituality of Relationship

A Simple Systematic Mariology

Praying Your Way through Luke's Gospel and the Acts of the Apostles

An Abecedarian of Animal Spirit Guides: Spiritual Growth through Reflections on Creatures

Overcome with Paschal Joy: Chanting through Lent and Easter— Daily Reflections with Familiar Hymns

Taking Leave of Your Home: Moving in the Peace of Christ

An Abecedarian of Sacred Trees: Spiritual Growth through Reflections on Woody Plants